Frozen Justice

Lessons from Bosnia and Herzegovina's Failed
Transitional Justice Strategy

Jared O. Bell

Series in Sociology

VERNON PRESS

www.vernonpress.com

In the Americas:
Vernon Press
1000 N West Street,
Suite 1200, Wilmington,
Delaware 19801
United States

In the rest of the world:
Vernon Press
C/Sancti Espiritu 17,
Malaga, 29006
Spain

Series in Sociology

Library of Congress Control Number: 2018946731

ISBN: 978-1-62273-687-4

Also available:

Hardback: 978-1-62273-204-3

E-book: 978-1-62273-597-6

Cover design by Vernon Press using elements created by flatart / Freepik

Table of Contents

List of Tables

List of Figures

Dedication

This book's dedication is twofold. First, to everyone from friends, family, and faculty, to other professional mentors who encouraged me to dream and reach for all that I could be, thank you. For all those who encouraged me to stay focused at times when I lost sight of the bigger plan and my dreams, thank you. I will hold tightly to this encouragement and warm sentiments as I move forward in my career. Second, this book is also dedicated to the hundreds of people in Sarajevo, Mostar, and Banja Luka who participated in this survey and to all those who were willing to meet with me to discuss life and politics in Bosnia and Herzegovina when I was on the ground. This book would not exist without your willingness to participate and share your views and perspectives. I'm indebted forever. Thank you.

Acknowledgements

I would like to thank and acknowledge the following people below, without whose input and/or mentorship this book would not have been possible: Dr. Ismael Muvingi, Nova Southeastern University, Dr. Dustin Berna, Nova Southeastern University, Dr. Cheryl Duckworth, Nova Southeastern University, Mr. Damir Jusić, University of Sarajevo, Mr. Denis Džidić, Balkans Investigative Reporting Network, Ms. Velma Šarić, Post-Conflict Research Center, Ms. Aleksandra Letić, Helsinki Committee for Human Rights in Republika Srpska, Mr. Muamer Šadinlija, Dr. Joseph Kaminski, International University of Sarajevo, Dr. Peter Plenta, International University of Sarajevo, Dr. Nathan Munier, International University of Sarajevo, Dr. Emil Knezović, International University of Sarajevo, Nermin Čakić, International University of Sarajevo.

Chapter 1

Introduction

Jared O. Bell

In response to the heinous crimes committed in Bosnia and Herzegovina and elsewhere in the former Yugoslavia from the early to mid-1990s the United Nations Security Council created the International Criminal Court for the Former Yugoslavia (ICTY) based in The Hague, Netherlands in May of 1993 to punish those who committed gross acts of human rights and genocide. The tribunals have heard lots of cases since its inception and have tried numerous perpetrators from the soldiers who carried out the killings to the leaders who orchestrated and ordered them. Despite, these successes, the ICTY and its mission remain highly controversial. One of the main major questions asked by some experts, scholars, and everyday citizens is whether or not this tribunal did enough to foster healing and reconciliation in many of the societies that were fractured by these conflicts. There are varying opinions on how to answer this question; many scholars will argue that the tribunals operated adequately within their mandate and with what they could to promote justice and reconciliation, while many who lived through the brutal wars would argue that there simply has been no justice. Bosnia and Herzegovina in particular still remains a country divided on issues of post-conflict justice among many other things.

Years later, a new government led draft strategy emerged in 2010. It was designed to be a comprehensive plan tasked to deal with unfinished transitional justice "business" and to promote reconciliation. However, the strategy has completely failed and there is currently no political will or momentum to revive it. But, did this strategy actually have any chance of being successful from the beginning? The purpose of this research was to explore this question by examining whether or not this strategy could foster reconciliation from the perspective of the everyday populace in Bosnia and Herzegovina, as well as explicate and analyze other elements surrounding domestic attempts at transitional justice throughout the country that may have contributed to this strategy's failure. The research discussed in this book took place in the form of a quantitative study which examined the perspective of Bosnians on the subject of the National Transitional Justice Strategy and reconciliation through a survey conducted in three major cities, Sarajevo, Mostar, and Banja Luka, where 487 participants were surveyed from June to August of 2015.

Many have asked me over the course of my academic and professional life, why I chose Bosnia and Herzegovina out of the many different transitional justice contexts that currently exist within the field. One answer is that I vividly remember the war playing out on television from even as far as Pittsburgh, Pennsylvania. The all-out warfare I saw on television perplexed me and frightened me at the same time. Naïve and not knowing any better I wondered if the United States could descend into such violence one day. When I decided to pursue peace and conflict studies academically, Bosnia and Herzegovina was one of the clearest cases that came to my mind with much curiosity and I found myself consumed with writing about the conflict and the post-conflict developments almost every chance I got. As I continue to conduct my research today, I believe there is still a lot to be learned from Bosnia and Herzegovina. The country is still transitioning to a full democracy and at the same time still dealing with post-conflict justice. But, the process has been frozen, as is indicated by the title of this book, by a variety of factors that this book seeks to explicate and discuss.

What is Transitional Justice?

Today, transitional justice is a quickly emerging field birthed from an array of inter-disciplinary studies ranging from conflict resolution to international development. The term transitional justice is defined as:

> a response to systemic or widespread violations of human rights. It seeks recognition for victims and promotion possibilities for peace, reconciliation, and democracy. Transitional justice is not a form of justice, but justice adapted to societies transforming themselves after a period of pervasive human rights abuses. (International Center for Transitional Justice, 2009, p. 1)

Developing transitional mechanisms and processes can be rather difficult and lengthy. In fact, Rhot-Arriaza (2006) notes that the term transitional justice itself may be misleading simply because the processes themselves may not take place in the immediate period after conflict. Moreover, she emphasizes the fact that transitions to peace and democracy may take decades. She also notes that some aspects of transition may take longer than others:

> [s]ome of the major factors societies must address are:

> "How much should they remember? How much should they forget? What should they teach their children? What should become of the leaders who orchestrated the discord and violence? The underlings who carried it out? The bystanders who did nothing to stop it? Where should they draw the

boundary between enough justice to destroy impunity and punishment so harsh that it becomes revenge? And how can they reunite communities where thousands of people have been raped, maimed, and tortured by their fellow citizens". (Stover & Weinstein, 2004, p. 2)

Such questions are wrought in a moral quagmire that is rooted in a search for justice and healing. Notions and concepts of justice are pluralistic and intersect with a variety of ideas, philosophies, and values. Justice, like beauty, is in the eye of the beholder and can be interpreted in a myriad of ways. For some people, justice could mean securing employment and a steady income, while some others may seek criminal trials, or official confessions or apologies (Stover & Weinstein, 2004). These societies are faced with vital dilemmas, such as how to implement a method of justice to which all members of society can ascribe.

Problems That Still Haunt Bosnia and Herzegovina

The first problem that continually plagues Bosnia and Herzegovina is that many political and social issues still stem from a lack of justice, accountability, reconciliation, and collective memorializing stemming from the 1992-1995 war. Moreover, one of the key issues in trying to create sustainable transitional justice mechanisms to deal with the past is that they have been extremely difficult to implement, gain collective support for, and has caused more political and social tensions than has fostered reconciliation. For many individuals in Bosnia and Herzegovina, justice has been a tiresome and overwhelming process. Even with the trials in The Hague and domestic efforts, for many, justice still seems to be elusive.

These notions inform the second problem, disillusionment. Many Bosnians are disillusioned by talk of justice and reconciliation and have lost faith in having any comprehensive process for dealing with the past, especially one led by the government. In a country where many of the same political factions who jockeyed for war some 20-odd years ago are still relatively in power and a plethora of development and economic issues exist, the possibility of sweeping post-conflict justice measures and complete reconciliation seems improbable currently. It is important to remember that transitional justice strategies are public policies, and they will not likely be successful without proper public interest and political support. How much political support can truly be garnered when the country's political elites attack the legitimacy of the rulings handed down by the ICTY and domestic courts?

Attempting to implement a method of justice that all of society can accept has been a challenge for Bosnia and Herzegovina. The conflict in Bosnia and Herzegovina that pitted neighbor against neighbor was the worst violence in Europe had seen since World War II and still has lasting effects today. It has been 23 years since the Dayton Peace Accords were signed and the conflict ended. Unfortunately, Bosnia and Herzegovina still remains a politically weak and ethnically fragmented state. Social reconstruction and reclamation have been slackened to say the least. In addition to Bosnia's divided state- and entity-level governing structures, the country's political power is further diluted by an extensive bureaucracy, which serves ten cantons, 149 municipalities, and the autonomous District of Brčko. Consequently, Bosnia and Herzegovina also lacks the social and political cohesion necessary to further post-war development and reconciliation (Moratti & Sabic-El-Rayess, 2009, p. 31). Moratti and Sabic-El-Rayess (2009) explain further that the lack of social cohesion rests on the fact that corruption remains high and trust in governmental structures and ineffective public administration remain low in Bosnia and Herzegovina today.

The authors also further explain that prior to the onset of the Bosnian war, the country's moderate level of economic development was coupled with an adequate social safety net, including health care and an educational infrastructure for its citizenry. The war severely slowed Bosnia's economic and social development, and post-war economic recovery has been primarily fueled by international assistance (Moratti & Sabic-El-Rayess, 2009).

The international community continues to push for a multi-ethnic state as the only viable solution for Bosnia and Herzegovina. Nonetheless, with the country's internal division along ethnic lines and the frequently obstructive behavior of local leaders, the international community has faced difficulties in rebuilding Bosnia's state institutions (Moretti & Sabic-El-Rayess, 2009, p. 8). In tandem with the European Union, United Nations, Organization for Security and Co-operation in Europe (OSCE), World Bank (WB), and other international organizations, the Office of the High Representative (OHR) has played a particularly important role in the development of political processes by applying polipressure in post-war Bosnia (Moratti & Sabic-El-Rayess, 2009, p. 8). As noted earlier, while the international community saw the Tribunal as the appropriate response to war crimes and genocide, domestically within Bosnia and Herzegovina, the process is extremely controversial. Members of the different ethnic groups that comprise the country feel in one way or another that the Tribunal targeted their ethnic group for prosecutions while the crimes of other ethnicities went unpunished, or some feel the sentences were too light for in comparison to the crimes that were committed. Also, the Tribunal has prosecuted higher level cases, leaving many perpetrators to the backlogged and ill-equipped Bosnian judicial system.

It is important to distinguish between judicial and non-judicial transitional justice. Before the end of the mandate for the ICTY, a War Crimes Chamber was added to Bosnia's court system. But, the process of doling out war crimes sentences has been extremely slow. Mallinder (2013) notes that the lower court system is also inefficient. Further, there is very little trust or faith in the court system to punish abusers. She further explains that the War Crimes Chamber of the Bosnian Judicial system is designed to work with local courts. The War Crimes Chamber is tasked with adjudicating on the most serious war crimes cases, while also having the power to refer the least complicated cases to local courts. She contends that while the bulk of the remaining cases in Bosnia will be tried by lower courts, they are ill-equipped to do so, due to a lack of resources, vulnerability to political pressure, and a plethora of out-standing war crimes cases (Mallinder, 2013).

She later explains that in order to address some of these problems, Bosnia's Criminal Procedure Code was amended in 2003 to harmonize legal proce-dures across the country and to introduce innovations to speed up trials, such as the use of plea bargains. However, these innovations have not been with-out their share of criticism, for example, many victims oppose the greater leniency offered by plea bargains (Mallinder, 2013, p. 63).

The author also maintains that non-judicial transitional mechanisms at-tempted (ranging from establishing truth commissions to memorialization projects) in Bosnia on local levels and by civil society organizations have largely failed (Mallinder, 2003). International scholars and academics have argued as to whether or not the true reconciliation and acceptance of the past is actually possible in Bosnia. So, it is truly fitting to explore the perspectives of Bosnians on the issues, especially as a draft Transitional Justice Strategy has been tasked to deal with "unfinished" business from the 1992-1995 war.

Introduction to the Strategy

As noted earlier, the draft National Transitional Justice Strategy discussed in this book was commissioned in 2010. The strategy was drafted by a team of 15 experts, chosen by the Council of Ministers, in collaboration with the United Nations Development Programme (UNDP), and it wrestles with the most sensitive issues in post-war Bosnian society, ranging from the establishment of the facts behind war crimes to reparations, memorials for victims, and institutional reform (Džidić, 2012, para. 1).

Moreover, the Strategy proposes the creation of non-judicial mechanisms to establish facts about the Bosnian war and to encourage people to come for-ward with their accounts. The five key areas this Strategy aimed to address in particular was truth and fact finding, institutional reform, rehabilitation, and compensation. The vision behind this strategy was to create an open, practi-cal, and productive dialogue about the past across all levels of Bosnian society so that the past is no longer distorted (Džidić, 2012). According to the strategy, the goal is to achieve satisfactory outcomes for victims and to build efficient, professional, and credible public institutions (Džidić, 2012).

To further this vision, the expert group put forward various proposals to the government of Bosnia and Herzegovina. "To give victims of the Bosnian war the right to "truth," the Strategy advises speeding-up the search for the 10,000 people who remain missing and creating a non-judicial fact finding mechanism, though the document does not discuss the mandate or form of such a mechanism" (Džidić, 201, para. 5). Other major goals of the Strategy include improving the rehabilitation mechanisms to overcome the consequences of the 1992-1995 war; or to establish a comprehensive and modern legal framework for continuous vetting of employees in public institution at all levels of government and that all institutions operate from a point of full transparency and accountability to citizens. Another key goal is to educate the general public and institutions about the importance of transitional justice in processes and institutional reform in post conflict societies. The strategy also boasts strategic goals for compensation in the way of both material and symbolic reparations.

During the drafting of the Strategy, five rounds of thematic consultations were held, participants of the consultations were representatives of the civil society organizations, journalists, representatives of religious communities, human rights organizations, women and other organizations dealing with gender equality issues, youth organizations, veterans' associations, associations of the people treated for post-traumatic stress disorder, representatives of associations and families of victims experts from relevant fields of expertise, and representatives of institutions at all levels of government responsible implementing the Transitional Justice Strategy (Bosnia and Herzegovina Ministry for Human Rights and Refugees and Bosnia and Herzegovina Ministry of Justice, 2013). A lot of emphasis was placed on having various civil society groups present because it was believed that civil society could be a bridge between the general population and those who were implementing the strategy at the state level.

The designing of the Transitional Justice Strategy took place in three phases. The first phase of creating a Transitional Justice Strategy, which lasted between April and July 2010, consultations focused on the situation analysis and identification of strategic issues and problems. During the second phase, which lasted between August and December 2010, participants of the consultations discussed relevant strategic objectives and activities as responses to the problems identified previously. During the third and final phase, the working group discussed impact assessment indicators, initial budget factors for the implementation of the activities required to reach the objectives and organized a series of public debates on the proposed Strategy (Bosnia and Herzegovina Ministry for Human Rights et al., 2013, p. 104).

It is important to note that this Strategy's development was not considered a panacea for all of the country's post-war ills and nor should it be. It intersects with other post-war strategies such as the Justice Sector Reform Strategy in Bosnia and Herzegovina, the Revised Strategy of Bosnia and Herzegovina for the Implementation of Annex VII of the Dayton Peace Agreement, the National War Crimes Strategy, the Public Administration Reform Strategy, and finally the Gender Action Plan and the Action Plan for the Implementation of UN-SCR 1325 in Bosnia and Herzegovina, 2010-2013 (Bosnia and Herzegovina Ministry for Human Rights et al, 2013). The section of the Transitional Justice Strategy addressing compensation as a form of reparations builds on that part of the Justice Sector Reform Strategy in Bosnia and Herzegovina.

During the consultation process, the lack of pro bono legal aid for victims of war when they are trying to exercise their right to compensation was identified as one of the key problems. For this reason, the implementation of the Justice Sector Reform Strategy in Bosnia and Herzegovina is important for the country to fulfill its obligations toward victims in terms of providing them pro bono legal aid services in support of their efforts to exercise their rights. Also, transitional justice is a sub-strategy of the overall Strategy for Judicial Reform.

Finally, according to the government appointed expert group, the Bosnian government would have spent roughly €9m on the Strategy; however, this amount does not take into account the full costs of the reparations program or the construction of memorials (Džidić, 2012). The Strategy calls for an implementation monitoring commission to oversee the implementation that consisted of representatives of the four key sectors: the executive authorities, professional community, the civil society and the Bosnia and Herzegovina Parliamentary Assembly. The executive authorities included one representative from each major governing body, the Council of Ministers, the Republika Srpska Government, the Federation of Bosnia and Herzegovina Government and the Brčko District Government (Bosnia and Herzegovina Ministry for Human Rights et al, 2013, p. 11).

The Strategy however, has not been implemented due to some major issues. Interest from political officials in both entities of Bosnia and Herzegovina considerably waned early on in the process. According to a report by the Ministry of Justice of Bosnia and Herzegovina (2013) immediately after its establishment, the expert working group worked in an efficient manner, however the absences of expert working members from relevant ministries of both entity governments, started to threaten legitimacy of the working group and actual complexion of the document (p. 35). This specifically relates to the representatives of one ministry of Federation of Bosnia and Herzegovina ministry and three ministries of Republika Srpska (Ministry of Justice of Bosnia and Herzegovina, 2013).

"Representatives from the three ministries of Republika Srpska Government stopped attending the meetings when EWG attempted to formulate framework strategic goals and when the representatives of the ministries of RS Government expressed reservations about the part of the proposed strategic objectives" (Ministry of Justice of Bosnia and Herzegovina, 2013, p. 35). Not too long after the Republika Srpska Minister of Justice sent a letter to expert working group and announced that a representative of that ministry will not participate in any more meetings, until Republika Srpska Government takes position about the draft of strategic objectives and adopts appropriate guidelines on how to continue the work with the expert group (Ministry of Justice of Bosnia and Herzegovina, 2013, p. 35). The expert working group held a few more public activities that aimed to engage various stakeholders in 2012 and in 2013 the aforementioned report maintains that the council of minister continued to debate the Transitional Justice Strategy, with the Republika Srpska still holding to earlier reservations (Ministry of Justice of Bosnia and Herzegovina, 2013). Following this period, very little seems to have been done or even reported on by official government agencies of the media.

What This Work Seeks to Do

The purpose of this study was to explore the perspectives of the general populace on Bosnia and Herzegovina's draft Transitional Justice Strategy and reconciliation. This study was designed with three main purposes in mind: (a) To gauge the opinion of members from the general Bosnian populace on whether or not they think their government can be implicit in fostering reconciliation among the everyday populace; (b) To determine whether or not people in the general Bosnian populace think that reconciliation is at all possible; (c) To examine and analyze variances between respondents from different locations, ages, genders, and ethnicities on the topics of transitional justice and reconciliation.

To this end there are four major hypothesis areas that guide the analysis of data collected for this book:

1. (Null) H_0: There will be no association between belief in the effectiveness of the Transitional Justice Strategy and belief that the Bosnian government's efforts will lead to reconciliation.

(Alternative) H_A: There will be association between belief in the effectiveness of the Transitional Justice Strategy and belief that the Bosnian government's efforts will lead to reconciliation.

2. (Null) H_0: There will be no statistically significant difference in the perspectives on whether it is possible for Bosnia and Herzegovina to move on between Bosniaks and Croats, and Serbs.

    (Alternative) H_A: Bosniaks and Croats will be more likely to believe that it is possible for Bosnia and Herzegovina to move on than Serbs.

3. (Null) H_0: There will be no statistically significant difference between those who believe that the government of Bosnia and Herzegovina can lead efforts toward reconciliation between respondents between the ages of 18 and 33 and respondents between the ages of 55 and 65.

    (Alternative) HA: Respondents between the ages of 18 and 33 will be more likely to believe that the government of Bosnia and Herzegovina can lead efforts towards reconciliation than respondents between the ages of 55 and 65.

4. (Null) H_0: There will be no difference in belief that the draft Transitional Justice Strategy's five key areas will be adequate in helping Bosnia and Herzegovina address its issues between men and women.

    (Alternative) H_A: Compared to women, men will be more likely to believe that the draft Transitional Justice Strategy's five key areas will be adequate in helping Bosnia and Herzegovina address its issues.

The Importance of This Research

As noted earlier, this research aims to contribute to a wide array of emerging transitional justice research projects to help us understand how to respond to human rights abuses and their aftermath. To this end, Palmer et al. (2013) notes that in the past two decades, numerous approaches to transitional justice have been advocated for and implemented. They elaborate: [t]ruth commissions, criminal trials, reparations programs, and commemoration initiatives are now routinely established in response to serious human rights violations. This burgeoning practice has been accompanied by a wide range of research projects, informing the design, implementation, and assessment of these justice initiatives. In many of these cases, human rights practice has driven the development of scholarship and certain advocacy agendas have profoundly shaped research. (Palmer et al., 2013, p. 19)

The field of transitional justice has grown exponentially from its roots in the political study of the nature of transition and the application of international law to these contexts (University of Ulster Transitional Justice Institute, 2013). Scholarship in this field now incorporates a broad range of interdisciplinary focuses which add considerable depth to the study of the mechanisms and processes employed by societies moving from conflict to peace and from repressive rule towards democracy contexts (University of Ulster Transitional Justice Institute, 2013). The University of Ulster Transitional Justice Institute (2013) reports, "[t]he inclusion of a broader range of disciplinary perspectives has also brought with it an increased diversity of theoretical and methodological approaches to the field and scholarship in general" (para. 1).

Both qualitative and quantitative methods have come to be used in assessing transitional justice methods. Pham and Vanick (2007) maintain that "human rights and transitional justice researchers often debate the value of either qualitative or quantitative methods, and sometimes of both of them" (p. 234). The authors further argue that

> a common mistake is to assert that either method is intrinsically superior to the other. The two methods have distinctly different purposes and should be seen as complementary. Research is not solely about collecting qualitative or quantitative data, but, rather, involves the strategic collection of data that will best benefit the objectives of the research and assist in evidence-based decision making for program and policy development. (Pham & Vanick, 2007, p. 234)

Pham and Vanick (2007) also argue that qualitative research offers a depth and richness of response that illuminates the dynamics of the process under study. The authors emphasize that in contrast, quantitative research methods entail the collection and/or analysis of data that can be measured numerically. Concerning this study, they note that in terms of transitional justice, quantitative data can be used to measure the frequency of support for various mechanisms and even to establish association of these attitudes with predictive factors such as exposure to trauma; qualitative data are best placed to describe what people understand by keywords such as justice or reconciliation (Pham and Vanick, 2007).

Pham and Vanick point out some very important aspects that are essential to understanding the research presented in this book and why I chose to use a quantitative method. I chose to employ a quantitative method because I wanted more of a general picture of what Bosnians thought about the strategy versus interviewing maybe 20-30 people to only get what I feel would be a small part of a much larger story. With the methodology I used, I believe I obtained many more perspectives. I do not disagree with what authors have to say concerning how often people rate qualitative or quantitative research as one being better than the other. This indeed is often the case, and researchers often feel that they have to choose one over the other. For this particular research project I believe that a quantitative method was the right fit because, outside of wanting to be able to get a much larger picture, I wanted to also measure and establish associations between variables. For instance, as I measured the association between ethnicity and the respondents' opinions on whether or not they believed Bosnia and Herzegovina could move forward as a country. I also believe that a quantitative study, in terms of this project, offers more substantial data that can be used to inform further research.

There are also debates in the field arguing that transitional justice research must be more practice focused in order to make results more empirical. Along these lines, Fischer (2011) argues that research needs to be practice-orientated and should generate policy recommendations; and at the same time, it must not create a set of blueprints that policy makers can use as for broad application for all contexts, since what is helpful in one context may be irrelevant or even harmful in another (p. 4). Fischer (2011) also maintains that

> "in order to achieve more reliable results, research has to involve, as much as possible, partners and actors from the countries in question. It has been recommended that views of the affected populations have to play a major role in decisions on how societies should deal with the past and that there is a need to listen to the people Action research can prepare the ground for this". (p. 5)

Kritz (2009) also notes that the more empirical the research, the better policy choices can be made when it comes to developing transitional justice mechanisms and policies. He further asserts that in this way, empirical research allows for the testing of the current assumptions guiding transitional justice policies (Kritz, 2009). Kritz's (2009) rationale for this is that "empirical research should be built upon to determine whether certain types of transitional justice mechanisms are more appropriate than others in specific kinds of transitions" (p. 15).

It is within these sentiments that the research for this book is rooted. There remains large gaps in empirical research when it comes to assessing transitional justice processes and whether or not they can actually foster reconciliation, healing, or even victim satisfaction. This book aims to serve as a springboard for discussion not only on the ongoing process of transitional justice in Bosnia and Herzegovina but also as one that can be used across other transitional justice contexts as well.

Overall, I believe this book contributes to scholarship on transitional justice and reconciliation in the three following ways:

First, by examining the Transitional Justice Strategy and its prescribed mechanisms and their impact on reconciliation in Bosnian society, one can learn more about identifying possible obstacles to reconciliation in all postconflict societies. While every post-conflict society is different, each case presents circumstances that can be used in contrast and comparison to another. In academic scholarship on transitional justice, scholars, experts, and policy makers do not always have to reinvent the proverbial wheel; they can use what they know to avoid certain mistakes or create successes when employing certain strategies and mechanisms.

Second, there are lessons to be learned by exploring the realities of transitional justice mechanisms from a theoretical aspect compared to the expectations of the people whose lives they are aimed at transforming. In understanding the difference experts and practitioners can ameliorate processes on the ground; after all, transitional justice mechanisms are aimed at reconciling people and societies. Therefore, it is important to know and understand how the people in a given society view a particular mechanism and what their expectations of this mechanism are in relation to their own reconciling. The more researchers can gauge and understand people's expectations, the better they can develop policies and mechanisms that are effective.

Third and finally, transitional justice discourse is enhanced by analyzing how gender, ethnicity, and age impact one's view on reconciliation and transitional justice mechanisms and strategies. The factors mentioned immediately above are extremely important when exploring how someone may perceive transitional justice mechanisms. By understanding more about how gender, ethnicity, and age impact views of transitional justice, scholars and practitioners may be able to develop strategies and mechanisms that are sensitive to this and therefore, may have more of an impact on fostering reconciliation and healing.

Chapter Overviews

The following topics of each chapter within this book will be discussed as follows:

Chapter 1: Chapter one briefly explains the transitional justice processes that have been utilized in Bosnia and Herzegovina and the country's struggles with moving on from the 1992-1995 conflict. This chapter also lays out the draft Transitional Justice Strategy of Bosnia and Herzegovina and its key functions. This chapter also lays out the purpose and rationale of the book and its contributions to the transitional justice field and its research.

Chapter 2: Chapter two explores different transitional justice theories and the mechanism the different mechanisms utilized within them.

Chapter 3: Chapter three explores the dimensions of implementing transitional justice mechanisms in a post-conflict society.

Chapter 4: Chapter four examines the nexus between transitional justice and its links to reconciliation.

Chapter 5: Chapter five gives a survey of pre and post war Bosnian history, which lays out some key important historic events that are important for understanding the political and social context of Bosnia and Herzegovina today.

Chapter 6: Chapter six looks at the processes of transitional justice in Bosnia and Herzegovina within the context of the International Tribunal for the former Yugoslavia and domestic progress towards transitional justice. As well as, offers an exploration of attitudes towards reconciliation and post-conflict justice and reconciliation in Bosnia and Herzegovina.

Chapter 7: Chapter seven explores the progress of transitional from other former Yugoslav domestic contexts.

Chapter 8: Chapter eight discusses the methodological framework that was designed for this particular study, including how the study was conducted, the selection of the sample, survey questions, as well as the data Analysis that was used.

Chapter 9: Chapter nine discusses the study results by looking at the findings from both the surveys and the hypothetical tests. This chapter seeks to connect some of the key theoretical aspects discussed earlier in the book with the aim, process, and execution of the Transitional Justice Strategy and how they impacted perceptions of it.

Chapter 10: Chapter ten presents a summary, conclusions, and lessons we can draw from Bosnia and Herzegovina's that can be considered in other transitional justice processes in the region and across the globe for policy makers, academics, and practitioners.

Chapter 2

Key Transitional Justice Theories and Mechanisms

Jared O. Bell

This chapter of the book gives an overview of key approaches to transitional justice: the retributive, restorative, reparative, institutional reform and hybrid approaches. States emerging from conflict have an obligation by international standards and norms to develop mechanisms that address the four key pillars of transitional justice: Truth, Reparation, Justice, and Guarantees of non-recurrence. States may choose a variety of approaches to meet these obligations. Which approach to use to achieve these obligations depends on the political and social context that emerges after a conflict. In some contexts, there may be clear cries for perpetrators or beneficiaries of human rights violations to be put on trial while in other contexts, some societies may choose to officially forget or seek to deal with crimes outside courts or tribunals.

Choosing a means of justice that every member of society can ascribe is difficult and as noted earlier about Bosnia and Herzegovina has been quite divisive. In fact, one of the major debates about transitional justice concerning war crimes from the 1990s in Bosnia and Herzegovina is whether or not retributive justice through tribunals was the appropriate means of dealing with the past. One can argue that clearly with the drafting of the National Transitional Justice Strategy is evident that trials at the ICTY simply were not enough to move the society forward.

Retributive Justice

Until very recently, retributive justice has received the most attention in conflict and democratization literature, and is also the type of justice, which is most commonly referred to by those skeptical toward post-conflict justice (Gates, Binningsbø, & Lie, 2007, p. 6). The theory of retributive justice emphasizes the need to hold perpetrators accountable and ensure some form of punishment for their crimes. It is a retroactive approach that justifies punishment as a response to past injustice or wrongdoing. The main justification behind this sentimentality is that the offender has gained unfair advantages through his or her actions, and that punishment will correct this (Maiese, 2003). Maise (2003) expounds:

> "Punishment removes the undeserved benefit by imposing a penalty that in some sense balances the harm inflicted by the offense. It is suffered as a debt that the wrongdoer owes his fellow citizens. Retributive justice in this way aims to restore both victim and offender to their appropriate relationship. It also acts to reinforce rules that have been broken and balance the scales of justice". (para. 1)

The institutional mechanisms for carrying out such justice include prosecution and sentencing in domestic courts and special tribunals, in international tribunals, in joint international and domestic tribunals, or in foreign courts (Schuttenberg, 2008, p. 3). Mani (2002) argues "that legal justice, or the rule of law as it is referred to here, and the entire apparatus of the justice system, is usually either delegitimized, debilitated, or destroyed during or prior to conflict" (p. 4). Hence, before it is possible to hold appropriate trials within the particular justice system, one would have to rebuild the required structures, a process which may take several years (Schuttenberg, 2008, p. 3).

Many post-conflict states are not afforded the luxury of lengthy rebuilding processes for a fractured or destroyed justice systems, as it may be of vital importance to address the serious crimes committed during times of conflict as early as possible so that society can start moving on (Schuttenberg, 2008). "As a result, this is why the instruments of retributive justice are most often tribunals. However, their use is not undisputed, as both positive and negative effects are possible. In fact, many authors describe tensions or even a trade-off between the goal to achieve justice and the goal to achieve peace. It is clear that tribunals cannot be the panacea to all problems regarding post-conflict peace building or reconciliation. These processes have to be adapted to the particular social, economic, cultural, and political circumstances and require many different instruments, among them reparation and capacity building" (Schuttenberg, 2008, p. 3).

Gates et al. (2007) note that in post-conflict democratic transitions these mechanisms are more likely to be carried out as part of the reconciliation process and as a response to violations human rights principles and standards. However, the authors argue that "in autocratic settings they are more arbitrary and usually directed toward the losing side of the conflict, such as separatist rebels, failed coup-makers, or leaders of the previous regime, in these situations, trials often take place as show-trials in which the outcome is known prior to the legal process" (Gates et al., 2007, p. 6).

However, many human rights activists and scholars within the democratiza-tion literature argue that there are moral and juridical obligations to hold perpetrators responsible for gross human rights violations, genocide, ethnic cleansing, torture, and other types of violent war-crimes (Gates et al., 2007, p. 6). Retributive justice may promote a new moral order by which the past has been addressed and grievances recompensed. Skeptics, however, maintain that justice for leaders of former regimes is likely to inflame tensions and exacerbate conflicts in ways that may delay or harm national reconciliation processes (Gates et al., 2007).

Since the end of World War II, beginning with the Nuremberg Tribunals (created to punish the Nazis for their crimes against humanity, war crimes, and genocide), there has been a rise in the use of tribunals. Tribunals have been used in, Argentina, Cambodia, Chile, and Guatemala to name a few. Retributive justice has also taken center stage since the International Criminal Court was formed in 2002 to deal with crimes committed by both states and individuals who commit crimes against humanity. The Nuremberg trials es-tablished an international precedent of justice and are often seen as one of the main influences in the establishment of the International Criminal Court for the former Yugoslavia (ICTY). The Nuremberg trials were a series of 13 trials carried out in Nuremberg, Germany between 1945 and 1949. "The de-fendants, who included Nazi Party officials and high-ranking military officers along with German industrialists, lawyers and doctors, were indicted on such charges as crimes against peace and crimes against humanity" ("Nuremberg Trials," 2010, para. 1).

There were many legal and procedural difficulties to overcome in setting up the Nuremberg trials. The major difficulty was that there was no precedent for an international trial of war criminals. In fact:

> "[t]here were earlier instances of prosecution for war crimes, such as the execution of Confederate army officer Henry Wirz (1823-65) for his mal-treatment of Union prisoners of war during the American Civil War (1861-65); and the courts-martial held by Turkey in 1919-20 to punish those re-sponsible for the Armenian genocide of 1915-16. However, these were tri-als conducted according to the laws of a single nation rather than, as in the case of the Nuremberg trials, a group of four powers (France, Britain, the Soviet Union and the US) with different legal traditions and practices". ("Nuremberg Trials," 2010, para. 4)

"The Allies eventually established laws and procedures for the Nuremberg trials with the London Charter of the International Military Tribunal (IMT), which was issued on August 8, 1945. Among other things, the charter defined three categories of crimes: crimes against peace (including planning, preparing, starting or waging wars of aggression or wars in violation of international agreements), war crimes (including violations of customs or laws of war, and improper treatment of civilians and prisoners of war), and crimes against humanity (including murder, enslavement or deportation of civilians, or persecution on political, religious, or racial grounds). It was determined that civilian officials, as well as military officers, could be prosecuted for war crimes" ("Nuremberg Trials", 2010, para. 5). However, the Nuremberg process was then and is still considered now to be controversial as it has been seen as victor's justice, which has been one of the main reasons for which the ICTY has been deemed unjust by some.

Restorative Justice

The next important theory to discuss is restorative justice in contrast to that of retributive. Restorative justice is rapidly being embraced throughout the world as an alternative that introduces new holistic justice processes and institutions (Llewellyn & Howse, 1999). Restorative justice is a conflict theory of justice that emphasizes repairing the harm caused by criminal behavior. "It is best accomplished when the parties themselves meet cooperatively to decide how to do this, thus leading to the transformation of people, relationships, and communities" (Prison Fellowship International, n.d., p. 1). Unlike retributive justice, restorative justice, as Zehr and Mika (1998) suggest, is tasked with healing victims' wounds, restoring offenders to law-abiding lives, and mending damaged interpersonal relationships and the community. Restorative justice is all-inclusive process, that brings all stakeholders together and allows opportunities for those directly impacted by the crimes in the process of responding to the pain and damage caused (Zehr & Mika, 1998).

Restorative justice is different from contemporary criminal (retributive) justice in several ways. First, it perceives criminal behavior more comprehensively; rather than defining crime as simply lawbreaking, it recognizes that offenders harm individuals, communities, and even possibly themselves (Prison Fellowship International, n.d., p. 1). Second, it involves more parties in responding to the crimes and the harms they have committed; rather than affording major roles only to government and the offender, it includes victims and communities also . Finally, restorative justice measures success differently; rather than measuring how much punishment is inflicted, it measures how much harm is repaired or prevented (Prison Fellowship International, n.d., p. 1).

Restorative justice mechanisms can and often do operate outside of established institutions such as courts and tribunals, retributive justice mechanisms. Restorative processes create space for parties to come together and discuss what may be needed for the healing and restoration of relationships and how to go about it (Llewellyn & Howse, 1999). Along these lines, restorative justice mechanisms can be employed for the work of justice during transitional periods (Llewellyn & Howse, 1999). It is also important to note that within the process, these mechanisms can also be used to develop new terms that can guide the post-transitional society's development, while at the same time parties craft a plan to restore their relationships (Llewellyn & Howse, 1999).

The process itself is long-term. Llewellyn & Howse (1990) point out that "[t]he importance and contributions of restorative justice mechanisms to post-conflict societies thus do not end with the transition. It is important to highlight that the work of restoring relationships is not finished when the transitional restorative justice process ends. In fact, it is quite the opposite; the restorative process is only the beginning of the work for restoration in that it identifies the steps required to repair the harm and restore relationships" (Llewellyn & Howse, 1999).

One popular restorative mechanism that has been used in post-conflict societies has been truth and reconciliation commissions. Truth commissions are established to investigate human rights abuses, perpetrated in a specific time period, usually during conflict and civil unrest (Mobekk, 2005, p. 266). Human rights abuses investigated by these commissions may vary in nature, from forced disappearances to mass killings. Truth commissions investigate abuses usually perpetrated and orchestrated by military, government, or other state institutions (Mobekk, 2005, p. 266). Bronkhorst (as cited in Brahm, 2009) explains that a truth commission is a temporary body, set up by an official authority (president, parliament) to investigate a pattern of gross human rights violations committed over a period of time in the past, with a view to issuing a public report, which includes victims' data and recommendations for justice and reconciliation.

Truth commissions allow victims and their relatives to openly discuss human rights abuses. Some commissions also even allow the perpetrators give their accounts of events (Mobekk, 2005, pp. 266-267). Truth commissions outside of tribunals have also been another major way for societies to address the past. One of the most notable truth commissions took place in South Africa. "As a result of decades of conflict in South Africa, parties to the pre-1994 negotiation process agreed that in order to deal with the challenges of the new democracy and face the future with confidence, the violence of the past had to be considered and acknowledged" (Maepa, 2005, para. 1).

These sentiments paved the way for The Promotion of National Unity and Reconciliation Act 34 of 1995 legally established the TRC. The Act mandated the Commission to deal with the nature, extent, and magnitude of the Apartheid conflict between 1960 and 1994 (Maepa, 2005, para. 2). The key objectives of the commission were to establish the fate and whereabouts of victims of gross human rights violations, and additionally grant amnesties to offenders who made full disclosures about violent acts committed for political reasons purposes during the Apartheid Era (Maepa, 2005, para. 2).

South Africa was not alone in its creation of a truth commission. Other notable truth commissions were established in East Timor and Morocco. There are many individuals who still argue today that Bosnia and Herzegovina needs more restorative rather than retributive measures. One such example of a successful local truth commission is that of the Srebrenica Commission, which will be expounded upon later.

Also, some post-conflict societies may choose to use amnesties, a process in which perpetrators do not face retributive punishment for their crimes. Amnesties are legal measures that have the effect of (a) prospectively barring criminal prosecution and, in some instances, civil action against certain individuals or categories of individuals in respect of specified criminal conduct committed before the amnesty was adopted, or (b) retroactively nullifying legal liability previously established (Office of the United Nations High Commissioner for Human Rights, 2009, p. 5). However, there are limits to amnesties; amnesties cannot be afforded to individuals who have committed serious crimes such as genocide or slavery.

Amnesties may be afforded to everyone who has committed gross human rights violations (outside of serious violations of international) which are called blanket amnesties or they can be conditional based on a set of criteria that have to be met by perpetrators of certain crimes before they can receive amnesty. An example of this is the context of South Africa, where those who applied for amnesty had to testify before the truth commission to have their amnesty granted.

According to Olsen, Payne, and Reiter (2010), amnesties have been the most common form of transitional justice throughout the globe. Some scholars note that amnesties may help the country move beyond the past by not dwelling in the past and also that amnesties do not carry the financial burden that some of the other forms of transitional justice do. On the other hand, other scholars argue that victims of past trauma may feel that the perpetrators got off free with no recourse or justice. Another prime historical example of an amnesty was when the Spanish government decided not to prosecute members of Francisco Franco's regime in the mid-1970s for their crimes in purging political opposition (Olsen et al., 2010).

Reparative Justice

Weitekamp (1993) explains that one commonly accepted definition of reparation is payment to victims of crime by an offender to cover losses incurred from a crime. Payment may take the form of money and/or services to the victim/s (p. 70) Reparations programs may be designed to give both material and symbolic compensation to victims. This is may include harms reparations for money or property, rehabilitation in mind, body, and socio-economic status. Reparations programs particularly, designate specific groups of victims as particularly as vulnerable and in need of immediate attention (International Center for Transitional Justice, 2007). This can include groups such as women, children, the elderly, certain ethnic or religious minority groups, etc (ICTJ, 2007). Some tough challenges of implementing reparations programs are quantifying suffering, classifying who should get what, and the cost burden it leaves newly transitioning states. An example of post-conflict reparations is when the Moroccan government awarded compensation to the victims of King Hassan II "Years of Led" repression. The compensation was awarded per the Truth and Equality Commission's (established by King Mohammed VI in 2004) recommendation.

Institutional Reform

Finally, many post-conflict societies work to transform their institutions so that the old order of past human rights abuses that led to conflict change, along with as the individuals who committed them. The International Center for Transitional Justice (2018) maintains that "Institutional reform is the process of reviewing and restructuring state institutions so that they respect human rights, preserve the rule of law, and are accountable to their constituents. By incorporating a transitional justice element, reform efforts can both provide accountability for individual perpetrators and disable the structures that allowed abuses to occur" (para. 2). The Center also emphasizes that institutional reform as a transitional justice method aims to acknowledge victims as citizens and rights holders and to re-build trust between all citizens and their governing institutions (ICTJ, 2018, para. 4).

Institutional reform can come in various forms such as structural reform and legal, lustrations, vetting, education reform, etc (ICTJ, 2018). However, institutions, two popular reforms are usually lustrations and vetting. Lustrations are policies that seek to cleanse or purge the government structures and institutions of the individuals or parties that were responsible for conflict, repression, or human rights abuses. Vetting is a process that may be used in tandem with lustrations or separately. Vetting is done to make sure that all those who are entering new positions in government or other state institutions have no connection to the former regime, conflict, or has benefitted from past human rights violations. Some scholars argue that lustrations and vettings may help in fostering widespread institutional reform and ensure that past abuses are not repeated (Stover, Megally, & Mufti, 2005).

A major concern of lustrations and vetting policies is that they may remove or block individuals who have the knowledge and experience (politically and economically) to move the country forward. Roos (2007) explains that the most positive aspect of lustration policies is that they are meant to create a sense of fresh air in a new democracy, that can lay foundations without the concern that people in high positions of power will try to undermine it. The author concretely explains that the aim of lustration is not to punish the allegedly guilty, which is the task of prosecutors but to protect the new democratic society. An example of lustration policies has been the de-ba'thification (removing of members from the Ba'athist party) of the Iraqi government after the ousting of Saddam Hussein to clear the new order of anyone who may have had ties to the former regime (Stover et al., 2005).

Hybrid Transitional Justice

Lastly, while it is easy to dichotomize justice, there has also been a more hybrid approach emerging around the world that utilizes different measures of transitional justice at once. Moreover, there must be an awareness of the distinction between national and individual reconciliation, particularly since different types of transitional justice mechanisms can advance one type of reconciliation more than another (Sriram and Pillay, 2005, p. 13). This sentimentality underlines the importance of implementing more than one type of mechanism to address past abuses. If reconciliation is reached on one level, but not on another, instability and insecurity may return (Sriram and Pillay, 2005). I argue that the proposed National Transitional Justice is a utilization of hybrid measures and mechanism to reach different levels of society from the individual level to the institutional level.

Rwanda has been a prime example of this where both tribunals and locally based courts (Gacaca courts) were used to hold perpetrators accountable for their role in the 1994 genocide. I believe that the transitional justice mechanism employed in Rwanda can be very much applied and useful in the Bosnian context as well. To elaborate, "[n]amed for the *Kinyarwanda* word for grass, *Gacaca* was a traditional form of communal justice, whereby communal elders would resolve disputes by devising compensatory solutions aimed at restoring societal harmony" (Powers, 2011, para. 4).

Powers (2011) further explains:[the] *Gacaca* proceedings took place on an *ad hoc* basis and encouraged community participation following the genocide in Rwanda in 1994. The Gacaca Law divided crimes into three categories: the first category, relegated to the exclusive jurisdiction of the national courts and the ICTR (International Criminal Tribunal for Rwanda), is reserved for the planners of the genocide and people who held positions of authority; Category 2 crimes include murder and bodily harm; and Category 3 is comprised solely of property crimes (para. 5). She further explains that due to the slow pace of the national courts, in May 2008, the Rwandan parliament transferred most of the remaining Category 1 cases to Gacaca, including cases of sexual violence. 120,000 lower-level suspects remained in Rwandan prisons, and the government soon realized it would take it over 200 years to try each case. It, therefore, passed Organic Law N° 40/2000 in 2001, re-purposing the traditional Gacaca courts to deal with the remaining genocide cases, so far it is estimated that over one million cases have been tried to date under this law. (Powers, 2011, para. 5)

However, the UN Security Council also set up the International Criminal Tribunal for Rwanda in neighboring Tanzania to prosecute those most responsible for the organized violence (Powers, 2011). The ICTR's main purpose is "to contribute to the process of national reconciliation in Rwanda and to the maintenance of peace in the region" and to prosecute persons involved in the genocide and other violations of international humanitarian law" (Steflja, 2012, para. 2). What is more, "[i]n addition to these officially declared purposes, scholars and policy makers have assigned a number of aims to the tribunal, including the establishment of a collective memory of the genocide, the foundation for a democratic order and a human rights culture, as well as the promotion of reconciliation" (Steflja, 2012, para. 2).

Conclusion

While this chapter of the book offers theories and mechanisms that have been established in the field so far, every day new ideas and assumptions are developing about transitional justice and what may be best to help victims gain closure and help societies move on. None of the transitional justice theories or mechanisms that I mentioned above are perfect, as I have lain out they each have their positives and their negatives. Some scholars, media pundits, policy makers, and everyday citizens are skeptical of transitional justice processes, for many some of these processes seemingly may not meet their expectations and yield the outcome that they hoped or desired for. However, no matter how imperfect some transitional justice mechanisms may be at fostering senses of justice and reconciliation among some, they are an integral part of helping transitioning states move beyond their difficult pasts. Transitional justice mechanisms or even strategies for that matter help establish a new societal order based on accountability, justice, reconciliation, and respect for human rights.

Chapter 3

Key Factors in Implementing Transitional Justice

Jared O. Bell

Beyond the complexities of competing transitional justice theories and mechanisms is the realistic aspect that must be addressed when trying to implement them. For transitional justice mechanisms or even strategies become an effective tool for moving society forward, there are some key factors that must be taken into consideration; transitional justice is not just propelled by wanting to know the truth or even give reparations to victims. Whether not transitional justice is implemented depends on both external and internal factors such as political and social context, timing, level of local ownership and interest, institutional, financial, and professional, and international influence.

Political and Social Context

Every transitional justice program design will be different depending on each country's transitional context. Each context depends on the society's societal needs, demands, and if the state has the capacity to meet those needs and demands. However, this process is both political and social in nature. As I noted briefly in chapter one, transitional justice is an inherently political process. There first must be actual political stability for a country to even proceed to designing transitional justice programs or strategies. If an impending conflict or even further collapses of governing institutions is eminent than any attempts at transitional justice are futile. Also, next to political stability transitional justice processes are often times at the mercy of political elites, who will decide if committing to post-conflict justice is in their best interests or not. This comes down to the notion of political will. Transitional justice takes political will to become a reality; it takes political elites and other domestic institutions to support the processes and which means allocating resources such as professional expertise and funding to the processes. This also means creating new institutions that aim to deal with the past, such as tribunals or a truth commission. New laws may also need to be implemented, for instance, laws may be needed to protect witnesses who testify against former perpetrators.

Also political elites must come to an agreement on what mechanisms should be used, as well as decide on who the perceived beneficiaries of human rights violations are and who the perceived victims are. Political will can also be limited to the demands of the general public. This is where it is important to consider the social context. Those implementing transitional justice mechanisms should carefully assess social contexts by looking at factors such as root causes of the conflict that took place and the identification of vulnerable populations, such as minority groups, women, children, and public sentiments (United Nations, 2010). Major underlying factors and the needs of vulnerable populations if ignored, maybe catalysts for further conflict. Political will can also be propelled from within a social context as well, especially if there is a demand by large segments of society who want justice and demand that the political elites create justice mechanisms and programs to address the wrongs of the past. Understanding the social context in divided societies like Bosnia and Herzegovina is even more important as it relates to transitional justice. As noted earlier, some transitional justice processes and mechanisms can be divisive and members of the general public may not have any interest in pushing their political elites to execute a transitional justice program or strategy that is perceived as victor's justice and unjust, biased, or unfair. Friedman (2015) argues that often times the state will have problems with how transitional justice and reconciliation are perceived due to a lingering bitterness that exist among groups who feel they have been unjustly targeted for retribution while those on the victorious side committed similar atrocities and go unpunished.

Timing

Timing is a very important part of implementing transitional justice. Transitional justice is seen as a process that takes place almost immediately after a conflict has ceased. The right timing may spurn the right amount of interest and political will to make transitional justice implementation feasible. Ultimately, transitional justice processes are limited by time. Evidence, victims, perpetrators, and witnesses may only be available within a certain time frame. Transitional justice is just as much about memory as it is accountability. Those who were at once involved in conflict or bore witness to it must be able to give their accounts to the best of their knowledge and ability. Waiting several years after a conflict has ended to establish a transitional justice process will not allow those who were once involved to do so. However, Barsalou (as cited by the University of Birmingham, 2016) maintains that it is beneficial at times for transitional justice to be seen as an on ongoing process. Especially in cases where implementing initiatives before society is ready can produce more divisions. For instance, she posits that there perhaps should be a delay in symbolic reparations like building memorials, until enough time has passed to allow survivors to come to a more balanced view about what took place during the conflict, so that memorials will not be divisive or one-sided (p. 13).

Level of Local Ownership and Interests

While the international community has spent a considerable amount of time, money, and resources in developing appropriate transitional justice mechanisms and processes that also aim to enforce human rights norms and standards across the globe, its role in executing local and domestic transitional justice processes is limited. Local ownership is an integral part of effective transitional justice initiatives. For transitional justice to be implemented successfully, it has to be owned by local institutions and society must have a general interest to spur enough political will to make it a reality. Many scholars and practitioners maintain that to build national ownership in transitional justice processes it is necessary to understand and integrate local populations at all stages.

This also includes academics and policy makers learning about local wants, needs, and preferences of transitional justice (Haider, 2016). When transitional justice is not owned, we risk it being viewed by the local population as imposed justice. As noted earlier, many argue in Bosnia and Herzegovina that the ICTY was an imposed system of justice by the international community, which some argue is the reason that various local communities throughout Bosnia and Herzegovina never felt any connection to justice rendered in the Hague and vindication for the crimes committed against them.

Transitional justice must be an inclusive process from beginning to end. This means that inclusive participation exists in all stages of the design, implementation, and evaluation (Haider, 2016). This is important not only in fostering local ownership of the process and perceptions of legitimacy, but it is also a chance for empowering local populations to be included in a range of decision making processes from local, national, and international levels (Haider, 2016). A major actor that is often implicit in fostering transitional justice ownership is civil society. Civil society can play a major role in engaging and empowering local populations to have their voices heard, monitor the transitional justice process, as well as serve as a buffer to disseminate information between state institutions and the general population.

Along these lines Duthie (2009) maintains that "civil society has played an important role in every country that has experienced a successful transitional justice endeavor. National non-governmental organizations (NGOs) have helped to initiate, advocate for, and shape some of the strongest and most interesting transitional justice initiatives that have been implemented around the world" (pp. 11-12). From Ghana to Peru, national and local organizations played major roles in shaping transitional justice mechanisms (Duthie, 2009). Transitional justice may also intersect with a variety of civil society organizations ranging from human rights groups, humanitarian aid organizations, victim and survivor associations, development NGOs, lawyers, academics, mental health and medical associations, religious organizations, and conflict transformation and peace building organizations (Duthie, 2009, p. 12).

Institutional, Financial, and Professional Resources

One of the most important factors concerning transitional justicue is the number of resources a post-conflict state may have available to give. For transitional justice to become a reality, a post-conflict state must have stable and functioning institutions; for instance, this includes a functioning legislature to make laws adopting transitional justice processes, a judiciary and prosecutorial offices to uphold and enforce these laws, and even a robust civil society to help propel demands for justice and accountability. Barsalou (2005) notes that the restoration of peace and security is a major security concerning transitional justice, for example, if judges, prosecutors, and witnesses fear reprisal, intimidation, or violence due to lack of proper security and policing then the process of transitional justice will be undermined. One of the key purposes of transitional justice after a conflict is to establish a new respect for the rule of law and which also includes security to enforce that new rule of law. Without proper functioning institutions, adopting transitional justice mechanisms, policies, and strategies that work and are successful have a slim to none chance.

Another key aspect of transitional justice remains the financial side; states must use transitional justice mechanism and design strategies that are both realistic and affordable. Realistic and affordable means that states should develop transitional justice goals that are within their economic periphery. Olsen et al. argue (2010) that all transitional justice mechanisms come with a price, but that all transitional justice mechanism do not cost the same. For instance, the cost of trials compared to truth commissions pales in comparison. Also, if a post-conflict state decides to give reparations of any sort to victims of a particular set of human rights abuses, regardless of if their material or symbolic the state must find a way to bear the brunt of the costs. For a society that is still rebuilding physical infrastructures, as well as social and political institutions, the cost of implementing transitional justice mechanisms added in can be overwhelming.

Besides institutional and financial resources, transitional justice success requires adequate professional resources as well. For instance, a state cannot promptly prosecute war crimes without well trained and knowledgeable legal experts. Also, I would like to particularly put emphasis on the point of well trained and knowledgeable legal expertise. Well-trained legal experts, whether they are judges, prosecutorial staff, or court employees, give both the process of war crimes prosecutions and the rule of law legitimacy.

Well-trained and professional staff demonstrates that the state is dedicated to stamping out impunity the best ways possible and that the new order of the state is indeed different from the previous regime that may have had flawed institutions which caused the society to break down and resort to conflict in the first place. The importance of professional resources goes beyond the legal sector; a post-conflict state may also need to have a strong and robust medical sector, staffed with professionals who can work with the remaining psychological damage victims may still harbor. Victims who may be still be traumatized may not be willing to participate in any transitional justice process if they feel that it will open old wounds.

International Influence and Interest

When it comes to the implementation of transitional justice, the international community plays just as much as an important role as some of the other factors mentioned earlier in this chapter if not more. The international community is the safeguard of international human rights, part of being that safeguard is putting pressure on states who violate human rights within their own borders to cease doing so and to stand up to impunity. Standing up to impunity means calling for accountability and justice for those who violate international human rights norms. This means that the international community has a huge stake in transitional justice and has largely been involved in supporting transitional justice processes across the globe, whether it is been through providing expertise or through financial support. Either way, the international community's participation, advocacy, and presence in post-conflict justice discourse, has been a cornerstone in transitional justice processes across the globe.

Olsen et al. (2010) explain that the role of the international community goes beyond just advocacy, organizational, and financial support to more indistinct roles. They further maintain that the concentration of particular mechanisms utilized in certain parts of the globe demonstrate that international factors may influence the application of transitional justice across borders. Perhaps if countries believe that they will benefit from international trade or aid, or membership in an international or regional organization by adopting transitional justice mechanisms, then they are more likely to do so (p. 79).

However, as we have seen through various examples globally, sometimes the international community has a particularly strong and committed interest in a particular transitional justice context. Barsalou (2005) maintains that "settings as East Timor, the former Yugoslavia, and Rwanda, the international community has committed substantial financial and professional resources to develop transitional justice institutions and programs, while other countries, such as the Democratic Republic of Congo, have received little attention and support" (p. 3). The interests of the international community in one particular transitional setting compared to another depends on a variety of factors ranging from the national interests of some key international actors to the ever-changing tide of geopolitics. Another key factor also depends on the discourse surrounding a particular post-conflict context also, international NGOs, civil society organizations, and the media play a huge role in mobilizing the international community on various human rights issues and the justice process thereafter. If these actors cannot raise enough "fuss" to draw the attention of policy makers, diplomats, and academics, then other contexts may go ignored and not get the same attention and resources deserved.

Conclusion

This chapter presented the realities of implementing transitional justice. Transitional justice processes and strategies do not just come to fruition because demands for justice materialize after a conflict. It is a process, and a long and arduous one at that. The demand for justice is only one part of it. States must have the capacity to answer those demands for justice. There is no hard and fast rule book for how and when a state develops these capacities. I know I have said this before, but, I must reiterate that every society goes through the transitional justice process at its own pace and time frame. While both the pace and time frame of implementing transitional justice processes may seem inadequate and frustrating to victims, witnesses, scholars, and practitioners, it is part of the milieu of post-conflict justice. In the end, despite how hectic, disorganized, disenchanting transitional justice processes may be upon implementation, they remain our only hope for standing against impunity and promoting human rights globally.

The factors that I laid out in this chapter are only some of many factors that should be considered. However, when contemplated upon, one can see the interconnection between the factors mentioned throughout this chapter, for instance, political will remains an important part at the center of transitional justice. If there is no political will or interests pushing post-conflict justice, then states will not be prompted to put forth the professional and financial resources that may be needed to establish and maintain transitional justice processes. No matter how inconsistent, the international community maybe when it comes to encouraging transitional justice in some post-conflict context and not others, this inconsistency, does not totally underscore the power and influence the international community has in terms of offering incentives that may foster the political will for a state to adopt transitional justice policies and strategies.

Chapter 4

The Link Between Transitional Justice and Reconciliation

Jared O. Bell

As established in chapter one, transitional justice is the process by which societies devise mechanisms and strategies to address past human rights violations, political repression, or communal violence. While societies most often build new physical infrastructure and governing institutions, they also create a new social fabric as well as address and reconcile the past, which is a very important part of creating a new post-conflict society. Transitional justice remains a complicated matter and many "scholars and practitioners agree that societies that have experienced violent conflict need to deal with legacies of the past to prevent a relapse into violence" (Fischer, 2011, p. 406). However, it has become clear that mechanisms aimed at promoting accountability do not immediately foster reconciliation and stability (Fischer, 2011). Fischer (2011) maintains that post-conflict societies need a combination of mechanisms, including legal justice and accountability, as well as truth recovery. She further argues that activities need to be undertaken from various levels (bottom-up and top-down) and need to address structural, behavioral, and attitudinal aspects, as well as the context, memory, and relationships (Fischer, 2011).

Understanding Post-Conflict Reconciliation

Before moving forward to discuss how transitional justice and reconciliation are intimately linked, it is crucial to explore the concept of post-conflict societal reconciliation. According to Clark (2010), "in the broadest sense possible, reconciliation involves the rebuilding of fractured individual and communal relationships after conflict, with a view toward encouraging meaningful interaction and cooperation between former antagonists" (para. 5). He further argues that reconciliation means much more than peaceful coexistence, which requires only that parties are no longer violent towards one another (Clark, 2010). Furthermore, non-violence may mean that the parties concerned simply avoid each other, seeking separation rather than repairing relationships (Clark, 2010). Yet, Clark (2010) contends that "reconciliation, requires the reshaping of parties' relationships, to lay the foundation for future engagement between them" (para. 5).

Along these lines, Fischer (2011) agrees that reconciliation is defined as a process through which a society moves from a divided past to a shared future. She holds that looking at the past in a way that allows people to see it in terms of collective pain shared responsibility may help to rebuild confidence amongst former enemies (Fischer, 2011). The author also maintains that the need for reconciliation is emphasized in particular for societies that have gone through a process of ethno-political conflict, as these are marked by a loss of trust, intergenerational transmission of trauma and grievances, negative interdependence (as the assertion of each group's identity is seen as requiring the negation of the other group's identity), and polarization (Fischer, 2011, p. 15).

Stover and Weinstein (2004) add that reconciliation must take place at the group level as well as at the individual level. They assert that reconciliation at the group level involves reconceptualizing identity, which means the revisiting of previous social roles, the search for shared identity, consensus about unifying memories and myths, as well as the development of cooperative relationships that allow for differing opinions and ideas. (Stover & Weinstein, 2004, p. 18). At the individual level, reconciliation may mean personal reconnection with friends and acquaintances from a former life (Stover & Weinstein, 2004). Transitional justice mechanisms help the process of reconciliation by beginning the conversation on both the group and individual levels. It is also important to note that mechanisms should be devised so that their impacts can be realized at both the group and individual levels. If reconciliation is reached on one level, but not on another, instability and insecurity can return (Sriram & Pillay, 2010, p. 13).

However, on a different note, Gibson (as cited in Chapman, 2009) argues that reconciliation does not require that people accept and embrace one another but only that they be willing to put up with whom they oppose. Or simply put, members of society only need to co-exist with one another. However, the main issue with trying to foster reconciliation in a post-conflict society is that the definition is subject to plural meanings. Chapman (2009) explains that "one reason for the difficulty in understanding the requirements for reconciliation is that the term refers to a wide variety of types and level of relationships and an equally broad array of initiatives to overcome ruptures in them" (p. 145). She further argues that "reconciliation is used synonymously with such diverse processes as peace building, mutual accommodation between former antagonists, and reconfiguration of individual, group identities, healing, restorative justice, social repair, and community building. Reconciliation is both a goal and a process" (Chapman, 2009, p. 145).

In Chapman's argument, one can observe the foundation for one of the main arguments as it pertains to reconciliation and transitional justice. As noted a few times throughout this book thus far, transitional justice mechanisms, while a means of fostering reconciliation, can also be a vehicle for furthering conflict and hampering peace. This is what has been coined as the "Peace Versus Justice Dichotomy." This dichotomy is that of post-conflict societies having to face the dealing with the crimes of the past so that they will not undermine the future. Yet paradoxically, the reality for such contexts is often a fragile and uncertain peace that could be disrupted by demands for accountability and justice for past wrongs (Llewellyn & Howse, 1999, pp. 9-10). Rigby (as cited in Ramsbotham, Miall, & Woodhouse, 2005) explores the dichotomy of peace versus justice by contrasting amnesia or a "forgive and forget" approach as one way of moving on for societies emerging out of conflict with the alternative of trials, purges, and the pursuit of justice at the opposite end of the spectrum. Ramsbotham et al. (2005) contend:

> "[s]ome societies can "forgive and forget" much more easily than others, and to achieve full reconstitution of relations between former enemies without having to go through the travails of justice, perhaps, for cultural reasons amnesia is chosen to be the path of reconciliation. Others appear unable to do so no matter what efforts are made by internal and external peace makers-only private vengeance, it seems, can re-ignite the burning sense of injustice". (p. 235)

However, it is also imperative that I convey that in most post-conflict settings, reconciliation cannot be obtained by transitional mechanisms by itself; it takes much more time and effort than any time-restricted trial, truth commission, or traditional process can yield (Mobekk, 2005, p. 271). He further contends that transitional justice processes are steps in the process towards reconciliation, not its achievement (Mobekk, 2005, p. 271). The process of reconciliation is a hard process to measure. No process will foster reconciliation between every member or group in society, and as is noted throughout this chapter, reconciliation means different things to different people.

Reconciliation, Truth, and Social Re-Construction

Moving forward, the ultimate link between transitional justice and reconciliation moves beyond justice and accountability; it is also about memory and identity. Reconciliation also means conflicting parties coming up with ways of what and how to remember from the past, and how these memories will impact the future of society; for instance, memorializing, symbolic reparations, and how future generations would be educated in the past. Social identity plays a huge role and factor in social reconstruction.

Societies must be willing to have an in-depth conversation to that involved opening up and discussing the "truth" or what Stone, Patton, and Heen (1999) call the "What Happened?" conversation. The "What Happened?" conversation, they argue, involves people in or who have just emerged from conflict, spending much of their time trying to assess what went on and who is to blame for it. Stone et al. (1999) present two errors that take place within the "What Happened?" conversation that are relevant to the truth in relation to transitional justice. The first is the truth assumption, "meaning that as we argue vociferously from our view, we often fail to question one simple assumption, which our whole stance in the conversation is built: 'I'm right and, you are wrong'" (Stone et al., 1999, p. 9). The second is the blame frame; the authors argue that the most difficult conversations focus significant attention on who is to blame for the catastrophe that has been created. Stone et al. (1999) argue that "talking about fault is similar to talking about truth: it produces disagreements, denial, and little learning. And that it evokes fears of punishment and insists on an either/or answer. Nobody wants to be blamed, especially unfairly, so our energy goes into being defensive" (p. 12).

In these two concepts, one can see the struggles societies face in initiating productive discussion or conversation on the truth after widespread conflict. For many, the truth becomes blurry, based on emotions, past experiences, and also a collective identity in which one shares with those who too have had the same experiences. As the authors note, it becomes difficult to see past one's own perceptions and ideas because, for many, one's version of the truth is very much essential to what the outcome or circumstances may be as a result of it (Stone et al., 1999). For societies trying to figure out how to assign justice based on this truth, it becomes complicated when it comes to determining whose version of the truth is viable, logical, and factual. Trying to decipher and translate truth for an entire society is tricky because there is a risk of alienating and ignoring one or more parties' side of the truth in favor of another's. This then may fuel already hot tensions between conflicting parties. Furthermore, in terms of blame, societies must come to an agreement on an established truth and the intentions of both the purported perpetrators and victims after a conflict. As the authors imply, blame is never accepted without reservation because it is often synonymous with punishment (Stone et al., 1999). Victimhood is also very subjective; therefore, placing blame is not so easy.

For societies emerging from conflict, it is arguable that an attempt at establishing the truth should come first in order to decide what should come next. However, as was noted earlier, every transitional process is different and does not always yield a truth that everyone can agree upon. Examples of this can be seen with the information that has been revealed from the ICTY and the domestic courts in Bosnia and Herzegovina; these processes established facts and truths that not everyone accepts. However, for many who have been victims or who have had loved ones perish the truth is extremely important. How else can an individual, much less a society, gain closure? An example, within the context of Bosnia and Herzegovina, is the exhuming of mass graves after the genocide. From testimony given at the Tribunals, exhumation experts were able to locate the bodies of many who perished during the war and inform their families. In turn, families were able to achieve some level of closure by burying their relatives.

Also, for post-conflict societies, deciding upon the truth becomes important when trying to figure out what to remember. According to Stover and Weinstein (2004), social reconstruction is a process that helps communities repair damaged social relations to a new level that they can consider normal. Normal does not imply that relationships or even that social habits will return. It means that the majority of community members can agree that social relations have reached a point that is tolerable.

In an attempt to find ways to help people heal and move on, memorializing is important. Memorializing helps societies create new collective social memories, which become a basis for restructuring and reclamation. Of course, I'm not naively arguing that a memorialization process based around established the truth is a panacea for fixing a post-conflict society's ill; after all, the established truth for some will never be the established truth for others. However, deciding what to remember and how to remember is a starting point for gaining common ground and working towards a shared vision of the future.

Conclusion

Transitional justice mechanisms alone cannot foster reconciliation in a post-conflict societal context. Transitional justice is only one part of the recipe for moving on. Transitional justice mechanisms and processes help society establish some level of the truth by having the "What Happened?" conversation so that victims can gain closure and so that guilt can be individualized. Part of moving on takes both individuals and communities to work together in creating a new nation and a new identity.

This part can take decades, after all, twenty three years after the war Bosnia and Herzegovina is still in the process of trying to create a postwar identity that moves beyond the brutalities of the war and a shared story that most can agree on. But, this process is still tightly connected to transitional justice, as Bosnians are still in the process of having the "What Happened?" conversation as their courts continue to investigate and prosecute war crimes. Having just the "What Happened?" conversation is not enough; it has been ongoing since 1995. Bosnian society collectively must decide what to etch into its collective memory; this takes both individuals and groups who are ready to recognize and accept some of the facts and truths that have already been rendered from the ICTY and domestic war crimes prosecutions.

Chapter 5

The History of Modern Day Bosnia and Herzegovina

Jared O. Bell

Bosnia and Herzegovina is a country that has a history filled with a wealth of rich culture and heritage that has come to create the multi-ethnic tapestry that the country is today. Over the centuries, this country has gone from a medieval Christian kingdom to an Ottoman foothold to a jewel in the crown of the Habsburg empire, and finally to a part of the Socialist Federal Republic of Yugoslavia. Sarajevo's old town is often called the Western Jerusalem because all three Abrahamic religions (Christianity, Judaism, and Islam) are represented there. In order to understand where some of the ethnic discord comes from, it is necessary to understand the history of Bosnia and Herzegovina and the region in more depth.

Around the time of the fall of the Roman Empire in 460 CE, Slavic tribes, including those of today's Slovenes, Croats, and Serbs, began migrating to the Balkans (Domin, 2001). Domin (2001) explains that "there is no agreement on where any of the Slavic tribes originated or why they came. However, it is thought that the migrants came from what are now Ukraine, Russia, and perhaps the Nordic countries" (Domin, 2001, para. 8). He further notes that they settled throughout the region in different places and developed differently as the three cultures evolved and he notes that even today Slovenians, Croats, and Serbs share a common ancient Slavic origin (Domin, 2001).

By the time of Emperor Charles the Great (c. 800 CE), the Slavs had increasingly settled in the region and became its permanent inhabitants; the region, called the Land of the Slavs or Slavinia, became modern-day Yugoslavia. The population slowly adopted Christianity, but was variously influenced by its two major sects from the outset (Domin, 2001). Slovenes and Croats converted to Roman Catholicism and adopted the Roman alphabet, while Serbs became Eastern Orthodox Christians and adopted Cyrillics to represent the same language (Domin, 2001).

During the Middle Ages, Bosnia was ruled by a series of foreign occupations from Croatia and Serbia, until it became its own independent Kingdom in the mid-1300s; the Kingdom then fell to the Ottomans in 1463. The Ottomans also annexed Herzegovina in the 1480s (Pinson, 2007). The history of the middle ages remains contentious among many in Bosnia and Herzegovina, and in the Balkans in general, as each ethnic group claims a connection to a great past. In the centuries after the invasion, a large number of South Slavs converted to Islam. The Ottomans did not force conversions, but only Muslims could own property, vote, or be elected to positions in government (Domin, 2001). Non-Muslims had to pay a tax (Domin, 2001).

Bosnia and Herzegovina remained provinces of the Ottoman Empire until the 1878 Congress of Berlin gave temporary control of the region to Austria-Hungary. In 1908, Austria-Hungary formally annexed the region (Pinson, 2007). In the late 1800s and early 1900s, nationalism began to take root across Europe. Smaller ethnic groups within these large empires were crying for more autonomy, freedom, and self-determination. The Austro-Hungarian authorities feared this happening in Bosnia and therefore, pushed for a united Bosnian state (which included both Muslims and Christians) to fend off nationalism and irredentism from neighboring Catholic Croatia and Orthodox Serbia, and the Muslim Ottoman Empire (Palmer, 2004). Bosnian Muslims saw themselves as a different and distinct ethnic group, while Croats and Serbs tried to claim them as their own (Palmer, 2004). In addition, many Serbs felt oppression in the Austro-Hungarian Empire, and the emerging Serbian nation state also laid claims to Bosnia. It was these claims that drove Serb Nationalism and encouraged Bosnian Serb nationalist, Gavrilo Princip, to assassinate Archduke Ferdinand in June of 1914, thus starting World War I (Bieber, 2014).

Following the war, Bosnia became part of the Kingdom of Yugoslavia (until 1929 Kingdom of Serbs, Croats, and Slovenes), which was a result of Yugoslavism, a form of nationalism that promoted Slavs in Southeast Europe after centuries of foreign occupation. Bieber (2014) notes that "[i]n interwar Yugoslavia, a centralist monarchy under the Serb Karađorđević dynasty dominated the country, resulting in widespread dissatisfaction among non-Serbs, whereas most Bosnian Serbs supported the state" (para. 7). The kingdom fell in 1943 during World War II, and Bosnia was annexed to an Ustaše-led Croatia. The Ustaše was a fascist regime set controlled by the Nazis. The fascist state committed genocide and ethnic cleansing against Jews and Serbs (Bieber, 2014). Many Serbs became royalist or nationalist Četnik under new movements in order to re-create a new Yugoslavia under Serb predominance or the Partisan movement, together with Croats and Muslims, which under the leadership of the Communist Party strove to reconstitute a Federal Yugoslavia (Bieber, 2014). As the Partisans led by Josip Broz Tito expelled the Ustaše from Bosnia and Herzegovina, it became one of the six federal republics of Communist Yugoslavia in 1945.

The Socialist Federal Republic of Yugoslavia

The new Yugoslavia was comprised of six autonomous republics: Serbia, Croatia, Slovenia, Bosnia and Herzegovina, Montenegro, and Macedonia (Friends Committee on National Legislation [FCNL], 1999). Post-war Yugoslavia was a socialist state based on the Communist party, the Yugoslav National Army (JNA), the police (or militia), and the concept of workers' self-management. For 45 years, Tito's totalitarianism quelled ethnic discord within Yugoslavia.

Because of its great losses during World War II and to prevent future bloodshed, Tito gave Bosnia a constitution and the status as an independent republic within the Yugoslav State, defined by its historic existence. As noted above, Bosnia in particular is and was made up largely of three ethnic groups: Serbs, Croats, and Bosniaks (Muslims). Post-World War II Bosnia became heavily industrialized as a result of Tito's military priorities (Wheeling Jesuit University Center for Educational Technologies, 2002). Many factories were built in Bosnia where they were close to natural resources and also safe from possible invasion.

Tito devised a political system within Yugoslavia that would not allow any one national group to dominate (Wheeling Jesuit University Center for Educational Technologies, 2002). He used suppression by sending dissidents to labor camps as well as banning national symbols and flags from the republics. Tito executed many of his opponents after he secured victory in 1945, and throughout his leadership, he imprisoned activists for nationalist movements (including Alija Izetbegović and Radovan Karadžić) (Domin, 2001). However, paradoxically according to Biruski (2012), Tito also quelled ethnic tensions by creating a sense of what looked like balance among the republics. He even acknowledged ethnic Albanians and their cries for more recognition by creating Kosovo as an autonomous region. In terms of Bosnia, Tito cultivated Muslims (Bosniaks) as an ethnic and religious group recognizing them officially as an ethnic group. By 1970, Bosniaks were the largest ethnicity within the Bosnian republic (Wheeling Jesuit University Center for Educational Technologies, 2012). Yet, there were sizeable minorities. Figures from the 1991 census show 17% percent of the population was Croat, 31% was Serb, while Muslims formed a majority of the population with 44% (Wheeling Jesuit University Center for Educational Technologies, 2012).

Between 1980 and 1991, the economic and political stability of Yugoslavia declined. Nationalist groups, including Albanians in Kosovo, Serbs in Croatia and Bosnia, and Croats in Bosnia, began calling for greater autonomy (FCLN, 1999). The major event that pushed Yugoslavia to its brink of destruction came on May 4, 1980, when Tito died. Many scholars have argued that despite suppressing ethnic tensions, Tito did very little to promote a Yugoslav national identity. Đilas (1995) argues that Tito was far from being a great unifier, and

notes Tito pursued many policies that eroded unity, explaining that in a "sim-
plistic, Marxist-Leninist manner, Tito saw nationalism as 'bourgeois ideology'
and national conflicts as caused by 'capitalism.' So after World War II, with the
'bourgeoisie' defeated, he did little to combat nationalism and forge unity"
(para. 10). The author further explains that while a common Yugoslav school
program was created, cultural exchanges among the six republics were not
very intense and with time became rare:

> [t]here was no university for all nationalities created, nor was there a poli-
> cy of encouraging students to study outside their republics. It was rare for
> a Croatian professor to teach in Belgrade or a Serbian one in Zagreb. When
> the media did advocate all-Yugoslav ideas, it was an exception to the rule.
> This cultural and intellectual autarky of republics helped preserve the tra-
> ditional nationalisms of various groups (Đilas, 1995, para. 10).

Regardless of the federal system in Socialist Yugoslavia, there was still tension
between the federalists, mainly Croats and Slovenes who championed greater
autonomy, and unitarists, largely Serbs. There were cycles of calls for greater
protest and self-determination (Jović, 2009). The central government's control
loosened due to increasing nationalist grievances and the Communist Party's
wish to support national self-determination in 1974 with a new constitution.
Since the Socialist Federal Republic (SFR) of Yugoslav federation was formed
in 1945, the constituent Socialist Republic of Serbia (SR Serbia) included the
two provinces, the Socialist Autonomous Provinces (SAP) Kosovo and SAP
Vojvodina (Jović, 2009). With the 1974 constitution, the influence of the central government of Socialist Republic (SR) in Serbia over the provinces was
greatly reduced, which gave them autonomy.

Attempting to ensure Tito's legacy, the 1974 Constitution also established a
system of year-long presidencies, on a rotation basis out of the eight leaders
of the republics and autonomous provinces. Tito's death would show that
such short terms were highly ineffective (Jović, 2009). Jović (2009) maintains
that his efforts essentially left a power vacuum, which was left open for most
of the 1980s. The 1974 Constitution replaced the office of President of Yugoslavia with the Yugoslav Presidency, an eight-member collective of representatives from each of the six republics and two autonomous provinces of the
Socialist Republic of Serbia, Kosovo, and Vojvodina (Jović, 2009). This greatly
diminished the influence Serbia had over these provinces, which led to resentment and rhetoric for nationalistic Serb politicians (Jović, 2009).

Economic and political developments from 1974 to 1980 set the scene for
the ruin of Yugoslavia and the beginning of a new conflict in the Balkans
(Domin, 2001). On May 4, 1980, Tito died at age 88 in Ljubljana, Slovenia.

After his death, there was increasing resentment of centralized government control. The state-run socialist economy continued to decline, as was the case in most of communist Eastern Europe. Nationalists demanded and called for more autonomy in each of Yugoslavia's republics. Crippling economic conditions fostered ethnic tensions, as nationalist politicians scapegoated blame for the difficult economic times (Domin, 2001). Increasingly, there were fears throughout the republics of Serb domination in the region. In the spring of 1981 clashes occurred in Kosovo between the Serb administration and numerous Kosovo Albanians calling for status as the seventh republic, but not for independence. This situation led to bloody and violent demonstrations, which were severely suppressed by the police as well as by tanks of the Yugoslav National Army (JNA) (Domin, 2001).

In February 1984, the city of Sarajevo successfully hosted the Winter Olympics—an international symbol of peace and tolerance. In May 1986, Slobodan Milošević, a former manager of a gas company, became head of the communist party of Serbia and stressed Serbian ultra-nationalism (Domin, 2001). A crisis in Kosovo propelled Milošević's transformation from a party underling to Serb hero (Ackerman & DuVall, 2000). In 1987 Milošević visited the province as tensions sparked between majority Albanians and minority Serbs. Near Kosovo Polje, the site of where Serbs had slain an Ottoman ruler in 1389, Milošević gave a fiery speech to angered Serbs who had battled with Kosovar police, saying that no one should dare beat them (Ackerman & Duvall, 2000). Their adulation convinced him of the political benefits from appeals to Serb nationalism (Ackerman & Duvall, 2000). On the 600th anniversary of the battle of Kosovo Polje on June 28, 1989, Milošević had an opportunity to clearly state his support for the Serb nation, demonstrating pure Serbian chauvinism by claiming tighter control over Kosovo (Domin, 2001). In March 1989 the autonomous status of Vojvodina and Kosovo was annulled, and those regions, against their collective wills, again became integral parts of Serbia. The dismantling of Tito's multi-ethnic Yugoslavia was underway (Domin, 2001).

The Bloody End of Yugoslavia

After Tito's death, Yugoslavia struggled to move forward. A rotating presidency was designed with 23 members from across the republics and the autonomous regions to govern. By 1990, all attempts to reconcile issues among the ethnic republics had failed and, with the addition of Serbia's push for more dominance, Yugoslavia's demise was imminent. In 1990, elections were held within Yugoslavia. Only in Montenegro and Serbia did the communist parties win, while nationalist parties came into power in the four other federal republics. The nationalist victories were in many ways a reaction against a fear of increasing Serb power (Domin, 2006). After the elections, Croats and Slovenians abandoned the idea of a unified Yugoslavia, left the FRY, and were recognized by European countries as independent states. "Franjo Tuđman, the new Croatian president, promised the voters a strong, democratic and independent Croatia within its historical borders" (Domin, 2006, para. 9). Serb President Slobodan Milošević argued that if Yugoslavia should dissolve, the borders of Serbia should be redefined because a future Serb state must include all areas inhabited by Serbs (Domin, 2006).

In June of 1991, Croatia and Slovenia declared independence, starting the domino effect of nationalistic self-determination and bloodshed (FCLN, 1999). Several months after the fighting in the republics of Slovenia and Croatia, the Bosnian war started and was the harshest chapter in the end of Yugoslavia. On February 29, 1992, Bosnia and Herzegovina passed a referendum to secede, but many Bosnian Serbs did not agree (Holbrooke, 1998). Under the guise of protecting the Serb minority in Bosnia, Serbian leaders like Slobodan Milošević provided arms and other forms of military support to the Bosnian Serbs. A prime example occurred in the spring of 1992, when the federal army, dominated by Serbs, shelled and slaughtered Croats and Muslims in Sarajevo, Bosnia's capital (Holbrooke, 1998).

The international community responded with sanctions (not always tightly enforced) to keep fuel and weapons from Serbia, which had (in April 1992) joined the Republic of Montenegro in a newer, smaller Yugoslavia. Also, throughout the war, the United States encouraged the UN and its European allies to employ a "strike and lift" strategy (Lynch, 2015). This meant that "[f]irst, the United Nations would lift the UN arms embargo on the Bosnian Muslims, permitting them to import weapons to defend themselves. Next, North Atlantic Treaty Organization (NATO) fighters would step up airstrikes against the Bosnian Serbs in an effort to prevent them from ethnic-cleansing Bosnian Muslims and to push them to the negotiating table. But the French and British governments, which had the most peacekeepers on the ground, were not willing to go along" (Lynch, 2015, para. 10). By August 1993, the United States finally persuaded the UN and European governments to authorize the use of air power, which did not start until 1994. But to secure backing from the UN and allies, Washington agreed that NATO would limit the authority for authorizing to then UN Secretary-General Boutros Boutros-Ghali (Lynch, 2015). For a while, the strategy seemed to be effective (Lynch, 2015).

However, throughout the country, Bosnian Serb guerrillas waged deadly campaigns of "cleansing," killing members of other ethnic groups or forcing them from their homes to create exclusively Serb areas (Holbrooke, p. 35). For instance, in the town of Prijedor in April 1992, Bosnian Serb leaders announced on the radio that it was taking over the town and the surrounding areas (Ahmetašević, 2015). Later on May 31st, Serb nationalists demanded that all non-Serbs mark their homes with white flags or sheets, and to wear a white armband when they left their houses. In the following months, Serb forces organized mass expulsions of an estimated fifty thousand Bosniaks and Croats (Ahmetašević, 2015).

According to Holbrooke (1998), attacks on civilians and international relief workers halted supplies of food and other necessities at a time when it was most important. In what became the worst refugee crisis in Europe since World War II, millions of Bosniaks and Croats were forced from their homes by July of 1992 (Holbrooke, 1998). Alarmed by ethnic cleansing on all sides of the conflict and other human rights abuses, the United Nations moved to punish war crimes (Holbrooke, 1998).

In early 1994, the fierce three-way fighting became a war between two sides when Croats and Muslims joined together to battle the Serbs. Earlier in the war, Croatian president Franjo Tudman also aimed at securing parts of Bosnia and Herzegovina as Croatian (Klip & Sluiter, 2001). The policies of the Republic of Croatia and Tudman toward Bosnia and Herzegovina were never totally transparent and always included Tudman's ultimate aim of expanding Croatia's borders (Klip & Sluiter, 2001). However, in February and March, the Muslims and Croats in Bosnia called a truce and formed a confederation, which in August agreed to a plan (developed by the United States, Russia, Britain, France, and Germany) for a 51-49 split of Bosnia, with the Serbs getting the lesser percentage. Despite what seemed like progress, the Muslim-Croat alliance, the peace proposal, and an ongoing arms embargo against all combatants, the fighting did not stop (Holbrooke, 1998).

In 1994 and 1995, Bosnian Serbs massacred residents in Sarajevo, Srebrenica and other cities that the United Nations had in May 1993 deemed "safe havens" for Muslim civilians. In the particular case of the infamous Srebrenica genocide from July 11 to July 22, 1995, some 8,000 military-age men, boys, and some elderly men were executed and dumped into pits in the surrounding forests (Taylor, 2015). The executions were well-planned, and the Serb army made considerable effort to disguise its activities. While the killings took place over just a few days, the process of finding the bodies has taken years, and the task of identifying and burying them properly is ongoing—more than 1,000 remain missing (Taylor, 2015). Neither the NATO air strikes mentioned above nor the cutoff of supplies from Serbia (as of August 1994) stopped the Bosnian Serbs, who blocked convoys of humanitarian aid and detained some of the 24,000 UN troops intended to stop hostilities (Holbrooke, 1998). With their allies in Serbia, Bosnian Serbs aimed to unite all the Serb-held lands of the former Kingdom of Yugoslavia. In September 1995, however, the Muslim-Croat alliance's conquests had reduced Serb-held territory in Bosnia from over two-thirds to just under one-half—the percentage allocated in the peace plan for the Serb autonomous region (Holbrooke, 1998).

In addition to the warfare, ethnic cleansing, and massacres, mass rape also took place across Bosnia. According to Human Rights Watch (1995) combatants for each of the parties to the conflict in Bosnia-Herzegovina raped women and girls in their homes, in front of family members and in the village square. Many women were arrested and raped during interrogations. In some villages and towns, women and girls were gathered together and taken to holding centers, often schools or community sports halls, where they were raped, gang-raped, and abused repeatedly, sometimes for days or even weeks at a time (Human Rights Watch, 1995). Rape by Bosnian Serb soldiers was systematic and widespread and has been deemed by some experts to have had genocidal intent.

Ending the War and Negotiating a New Bosnia and Herzegovina

Finally, the general framework agreement for peace, known as the Dayton Accords, which ended the almost four-year war in Bosnia, was reached on November 21, 1995, after three weeks of negotiations by the then Serbian President Slobodan Milošević, Bosnia and Herzegovina President Alija Izetbegović, and President of Croatia Franjo Tuđman (Ozturk, 2012). Understanding this negotiation process as it relates to the end of the war and the creation of the modern-day Bosnia and Herzegovina will help elucidate the many reasons why conflict still persists in Bosnia today.

After a series of earlier failed peace talks, negotiations and proposals were led by former US secretary Cyrus Vance and British Foreign Secretary Lord David Owen. The Clinton administration developed a policy called "Endgame," which was a strategy that laid out a comprehensive plan to end the war and atrocities immediately (Daalder, 2000). To lead this mammoth task Clinton appointed former US Ambassador to Germany, Richard Holbrooke, who had extensive diplomatic experience to serve as chief mediator and negotiator throughout the emerging peace talks (Daalder, 2000). Holbrooke's renowned reputation for toughness, tenacity, and "bulldozing" bluntness coupled with the fact that he had already spent hundreds of hours dealing with key figures and understood their strengths, weaknesses, and personalities, hinted that he might be effective in ending the long-standing war (Daalder, 2000).

The first step that Holbrooke took was to "unify" the West by subordinating key European players to US control of the process. Before Holbrooke entered the negotiation stage, representatives of the US, the UK, France, Germany, Italy, Greece, and Russia had formed the so-called "Contact Group" to address the Balkan crisis (Holbrooke, 1998). Although negotiations within the Contact Group were difficult and extremely divisive at times, by skillfully making use of this forum, Holbrooke was able to unify positions and to obtain NATO's military support for his negotiation effort (Holbrooke, 1998). The Europeans were not really in the position to challenge US leadership in this new negotiation effort, given the failure of previous European-led initiatives (Holbrooke, 1998). Cohen (1993) explains that European reluctance to support a military intervention with clear political goals proved to be the main obstacle in securing a settlement. Cohen (1993) further explains that the litany of European failures is astonishing—numerous cease-fire agreements were broken and none of the main commitments undertaken by the Serb side were respected. Moreover, as another key tactic, Holbrooke also took advantage of the newly formed Muslim-Croat Federation. This coalition was a highly fragile entity because of the numerous differences between the Bosnian Croats and the Bosnian Muslims. Yet, Holbrooke strongly encouraged its maintenance, since he knew that a unified opposition to the Serbs was essential in order to equalize the balance of power and accelerate the ripening process (Holbrooke, 1998).

Finally, Holbrooke sought to confront the Bosnian Serbs' intransigence by persuading the Serbian President Slobodan Milošević, who was experiencing substantial economic and political pressure from international sanctions, to use his influence over them. In doing so, Holbrooke was able to unify the Serb front. From that point on, Milošević would speak for Bosnian Serbs. This obviously infuriated the Bosnian Serb leaders, who were nonetheless powerless to overtake Milošević's "authority." Moreover, aware of the difficulties of negotiating very divisive issues from the beginning, Holbrooke adopted what Watkins (2003) calls "a split and-sequence logic strategy," dividing the agenda into subsets and negotiating the subsets: Serbia, Croatian Serbs, Croatia Fractions, Bosnia, Bosnian Serbs, Bosnian Muslims, Bosnian Croats, Russia, US Administration and Congress, NATO, UN, EU, France, Germany, UK, Italy, and Greece. Holbrooke believed that he had to approach this negotiation piecemeal and step-by-step, locking in his win as he went along (Watkins, 2003).

"Hence, his first goal was to obtain agreement on a set of principles that dealt primarily with basic institutional arrangements: Recognizing Bosnia's existing borders, accepting the creation of two entities within Bosnia—one for the Bosnian Muslims and Croats and one for the Bosnian Serbs, allowing each entity to establish relationships with neighboring countries, and asserting a commitment to basic human rights" (Casmir, Diechtiareff, Letica, & Switzer, 2005, p. 14). Although many administration officials criticized Holbrooke for not negotiating a ceasefire earlier on, Holbrooke maintained that seeking a cease-fire that early in the process could have repercussions on securing the ultimate goal of lasting peace in Bosnia and Herzegovina. Holbrooke's next goal was ending the siege of Sarajevo (Casmir et al., 2005). "By making clear to the Serb leaders that the NATO bombing campaign would continue unless they agreed to discuss an end to the siege, he forced them to sign a withdrawal agreement" (Casmir et al., 2005, p. 14). The third and final step he took was to seek agreement on a second set of principles that would define how the two entities within Bosnia fuse together, by establishing a governmental superstructure (Casmir et al., 2005). The final signed agreement established, among other things, definitions of the unifying structures that governed Bosnia and Herzegovina, a commitment to free democratic elections under international supervision in both entities, and a pledge to allow the international community to monitor compliance and implementation of the agreement (Casmir et al., 2005).

At that point, Holbrooke was convinced that it was time to seek a cease-fire agreement. But, the Bosnian Muslims suddenly became unwilling to negotiate because they felt they could win on the battleground. President Izetbegović insisted that his troops would not lay down their arms (Casmir et al., 2005). In order for Holbrooke to secure a cease-fire he had to use pressures and incentives in order to alter the Muslims' perception of their reality and to convince them that the agreement was their preferred alternative (Casmir et al., 2005).

Throughout the process, he continued to remind the leaders that this was their last chance to end the war with the help of the United States and the international community; Holbrooke and his team were eventually able to convince each leader to concede some parts of land for the sake of ending the war and obtaining peace in the region (Casmir et al., 2005). They all knew this was in their long-term interests because their citizens were suffering and they were at a mutual stalemate (Casmir et al., 2005).

In addition to ending the war and dividing up land, the agreement created a governance structure that recognized all warring ethnic groups as active parties (Ahmetašević, 2015). As noted earlier, Dayton created a complex multi-layered system of: two administrative entities (Republika Srpska and the Federation of Bosnia and Herzegovina), three presidents, and ten cantons, each with its own president, ministries, and parliament (Ahmetašević, 2015). With the final details finalized on December 14, 1995, the agreement was signed, after about 100,000 people had died and more than three million others had become refugees. At the time NATO troops numbering around 60,000 entered Bosnia to enforce the accords (Holbrooke, 1998).

Conclusion

Understanding the historical and political background sheds light on the current state of Bosnia and Herzegovina. One simply cannot grasp the process of a transitioning state without following the complex history of it. It is impossible to begin to understand the current political system in Bosnia and Herzegovina without understanding why it was constructed this way after the conflict. Understanding the historical developments of Bosnia and Herzegovina allows us to place the political discord and dysfunction that is alluded to in the preceding chapter and also gives us a sense as to why implementing transitional justice or even major reforms has been difficult. The ongoing conflict between the country's political elites is not just current; it is based in recent history. As noted earlier, the international community developed a power-sharing mechanism to stop the war in and help steer the country towards democracy and lasting peace. However, this system has entrenched the divisions from once warring factions into Bosnia and Herzegovina's political system, a system which again allows for gridlock when political elites lack the desire or interests to cooperate. In the end, this gridlock stifles progressive change and blocks the country from accomplishing much-needed reforms and policies.

Chapter 6

Transitional Justice, Reconciliation, and Bosnia and Herzegovina

Jared O. Bell

Now that some of the theoretical aspects of transitional justice and the historical background have been discussed, it is appropriate to address transitional justice within the context of Bosnia and Herzegovina in relation the International Criminal Tribunal for the former Yugoslavia (ICTY). The ICTY has been the leading effort in dealing with war crimes in Bosnia and Herzegovina and other former Yugoslav countries. The ICTY was established in May of 1993 as a temporary institution, set up for the specific purpose of investigating crimes committed during the wars in the former Yugoslavia and prosecuting those responsible (International Criminal Tribunal for the Former Yugoslavia, 2010, para. 1). This was done at a time when the domestic judicial systems in the former Yugoslavia were not able or willing to do so themselves (International Criminal Tribunal for the Former Yugoslavia, 2010, para. 1).

The ICTY was the first Tribunal established under Chapter VII of the UN Charter as a means of maintaining international peace and security. It is based on the SC Resolution 827 passed and was the first international criminal court to enforce the existing body of international humanitarian law (Lescure, 1996, p. 5). The tribunal was solely established to deal with certain offenses committed on the territory of the former Yugoslavia since 1991 (Lescure, 1996, p. 5). The ICTY ceased operation on December 21, 2017, after 24 years.

The Statute of the International Criminal Tribunal for the Former Yugoslavia states that the ICTY shall have "the power to prosecute persons responsible for serious violations of international humanitarian law that are defined as: Grave breaches of the Geneva Convention of 1949 [Article 2], violations of the laws or customs of war [Article 3], genocide [Article 4], and crimes against humanity [Article 5]" (Lescure, 1996, p. 5). Article 9 establishes that the Tribunal shall have primacy over national courts whereas Article 11 describes its organs, namely the chambers (three trial chambers and an appeals chamber), the prosecutor and a registry servicing both the chamber and the prosecutor (Lescure, 1996, p. 5).

During its operation, 161 individuals were indicted. 90 were sentenced, 56 served their sentence, 19 were acquitted, and 13 cases were referred to national jurisdiction. (ICTY, 2017). "The ICTY is the first international tribunal after World War II to hold high-level leaders accountable for their crimes" (ICTY, 1995, p. 1). "The ICTY indicted a head of state (while still in office), prime ministers, army chiefs-of-staff, interior ministers, and many other high and mid-level political, military, and police leaders from all sides of the conflict" (ICTY, 1995, p. 1). "Some individuals, such as the former Herzeg-Bosnia (an illegitimate Croat-controlled territory during the war) Vice-President, Dario Kordić, have been convicted and are serving their sentences" (ICTY, 1995, p. 1).

About 4,650 witnesses have told their stories in court (ICTY, 2017). Through this, they have contributed to creating elements of a historical record. In addition to those who have testified, the Tribunal's prosecution has also interviewed many other potential witnesses (ICTY, 2006, p. 4). This gave some victims and witnesses a real sense that they and their communities were involved in the Tribunal's work.

However, outside of this, as previously discussed, critics have questioned whether the tribunal exacerbates tensions rather than promotes reconciliation, as is claimed by tribunal supporters. A few years into its existence polls showed a generally negative reaction to the tribunal amongst the Serb and Croat public (Lescure, 1996, p. 57). "The majority of Croats and Serbs doubted the tribunal's integrity and question the tenability of its legal procedures (although the Serbian and Croatian opinions of the court are almost always exactly the opposite with regard to the cases that involve both ethnic groups)" (Lescure, 1996, p. 57). While Kosovo Albanians and Bosnian Muslims, on the other hand, expressed their respect for the court and believed in its impartiality, but their feelings seemingly often changed when their own individuals stood accused of committing atrocities against opponents (Lescure, 1996, p. 57).

Moreover, "some three-quarters of those indicted thus far have been Serbs (or Montenegrins), to the extent that the majority Bosnian Serb and Serbian political and military leaderships have been indicted, while there have been far fewer indictments resulting from crimes committed against Serbs" (Lescure, 1996, p. 57). Critics saw the tribunal as operating under a major bias, while defenders of the tribunal saw this as indicative of the heinousness of the crimes committed (Lesecure, 1996, p. 57).

Beyond this, Hoare (2008) argues that "with no driving idea of which side was to blame, which of its leaders had orchestrated the mass murder, and who should, therefore, be punished, the ICTY prosecution proceeded to indict individual suspects on a piecemeal, haphazard basis, beginning with lower level figures and largely leaving the top leadership of Serbia untouched" (para. 10). He also emphatically maintains that not only did the ICTY have no mandate to prosecute crimes of aggression, but that prosecutions were largely for crimes committed by the perpetrators within their own state, rather than against the inhabitants of neighboring states (Hoare, 2008, para. 10). This means that those persons largely responsible for crimes committed across borders never were fully held responsible for committing war crimes and violating states' sovereignty. Hoare (2008) also argues that the ICTY was the product of concession, compromise, and collaboration, not of victory and the desire for retribution (para. 10). The ICTY was not imposed by the victims, but by outside powers over both victims and aggressors alike (Hoare, 2008, para. 10).

Stover and Weinstein (2004) also offer some insight into the question of the justice and the legitimacy of the ICTY. The authors note that although the vast majority of witnesses they had interviewed supported war crimes trials, they were far less certain about whether justice had been rendered in the cases in which they testified. In addressing the witnesses, Stover and Weinstein (2004) write, "tribunal Justice, they said, was capricious, unpredictable, and inevitably incomplete: defendants could be acquitted; sentences could be trifling, even laughable, given the enormity of the crimes; and verdicts could be overturned" (p. 115).

The authors also note that justice for many witnesses also meant piercing the veil of denial about past war crimes that had hovered over their divided community since the war. Many felt betrayed by neighbors of other ethnic groups who supported radical nationalist leaders or had aided and abetted paramilitary groups. Stover and Weinstein (2004), hold "[f]or many witnesses, reconciliation would only take hold once their neighbors from the opposing group had acknowledged their complicity in war crimes" (p. 115).

However, Meernik and Guerrero (2014) present another side to the argument about the legitimacy of the ICTY on an individual level. They note that, while it has been proven without a reasonable doubt that the ICTY has not fostered societal reconciliation, its work can still have benefits among individual reconciliation throughout Bosnia. The authors offer three key reasons for their opinion: First that the judgments can aid in establishing legal and historical truths that can contribute to the reconciliation process. Second, by finding individuals guilty of planning and ordering human rights atrocities and not whole ethnic groups may reduce the need for vengeance or retribution. And third, that its findings and outreach work during and after operation in Bosnia and Herzegovina provides individuals of various ethnic communities opportunities to explore the past together (Meernik and Guerrero, 2014, p. 389).

Yet, despite Meernik and Guerrero's positive introspection on the ICTY's work, the year 2017 with its series of high profile war crimes convictions, proved that divisions over the ITCY and its convictions abound. In November 2017, these sentiments were still present as Bosnian Serb Army General Ratko Mladić was convicted of committing crimes and genocide for his role in the Srebrenica genocide. Bosniaks celebrated the former general's conviction, while Serbs called him a hero and honored him as such. Mladić's conviction was not the only one who showed that there remain conflicted ideas and opinions on who gets termed a war criminal and who doesn't. Bosnian Croat general Slobodan Praljak, who was convicted of committing war crimes and crimes against Bosniak civilians in the then-Croat led breakaway faction of Herzeg-Bosnia, committed suicide during his trial on November 29, 2017, and thereafter was celebrated as a hero and a martyr by Croats in both Bosnia and Croatia. It is instances such as these which continue to sow divisions as members of different ethnic groups grapple with the realities of the war, who is responsible, and who should be held accountable. Despite the abundance of information obtained and disseminated through the ICTY, there are many who are not yet ready to accept the truths that the information has yielded. Nor has it particularly bought person across Bosnia and Herzegovina together to figure out how to collectively acknowledge the truth as Meernik and Guerero suggest.

Domestic Transitional Justice Initiatives and Mechanisms within Bosnia and Herzegovina

Despite the work of the ICTY, there has been a variety of domestic transitional justice mechanisms attempted in Bosnia and Herzegovina, but many have continued to be seen as ineffective and have failed. Some efforts have been judicial and others have been non-judicial. According to Mallinder (2013), so far there have been only limited non-judicial forms of transitional justice and Bosnian civil society remains comparatively weak. There are over a thousand civil society and victims' groups in Bosnia and Herzegovina and many remain underfunded, lacking in expertise, and often disconnected from everyday citizens. Nonetheless, some victims' associations and civil society groups have engaged in ad hoc grassroots transitional justice endeavors, including memorialization, truth-telling, and psychosocial healing. These measures have, however, been piecemeal and rarely reached across ethnic boundaries (Mallinder, 2013). One major issue is despite the positive things that civil society may do during transitional justice or any other endeavor for that matter is that many efforts go uncoordinated. Often there will be more than one civil society organization trying to design or implement similar projects or programs at the same time. Often no agreement has been sought to cooperate or even consult with organizations possibly doing the same things.

In terms of government-led non-judicial transitional justice mechanisms, Rangelov and Theros (2007) noted that a truth-telling commission for Bosnia has been in the works for years, but nothing has ever materialized. As noted earlier in this literature review, the one successful example of a local truth commission in Bosnia and Herzegovina is the Srebrenica Commission in the Republika Srpska with its final report released in 2004. The report established that from July 10-19, 1995, 7,800 Bosniak men and boys were executed by the forces of the Republika Srpska Army. The Commission also discussed how the perpetrators moved the bodies to secondary graves in order to conceal their crimes (Kostić, 2012). The author goes on to explain that:

> [g]uided by information from sources in Republika Srpska, the Commission was able to discover 32 gravesites. Finally, it established the structure of the military forces participating in the massacres, and created an identity database of those who perished in the massacres. The work of the Commission resulted in an official apology by the Government of Republika Srpska to the Bosniaks of Srebrenica on 10 November 2004. In its apology, the Government of Republika Srpska acknowledged that a massive crime had taken place during the Republika Srpska Army offensive on Srebrenica in 1995, and expressed its readiness to face up to the tragic events of the war in Bosnia and Herzegovina. (Kostić, 2012, p. 662)

A program dealing with financial reparations has yet to actually materialize, according to the author, because there is a lack of any real substantive discussion domestically or international. Politically and judicially, vetting also took place initially within Bosnia and Herzegovina. According to Mallinder (2013), the need to bar individuals who were responsible for atrocities committed during the war from accessing political power was acknowledged in the Dayton Accords, which articulated that persons convicted of war crimes or those who were fugitives from war crimes indictments are banned from serving in office (p. 64).

Furthermore, the accords empowered the Office of the High Representative (OHR) to remove civil servants from public office for offenses varying from wartime crimes to obstructing the peace (Mallinder, 2013). "Under this process 185 public officials were removed from office, including senior officials and politicians, although some of these individuals have now been "rehabilitated" by the OHR, which means that the OHR has decided to allow them to reenter public life" (Mallinder, 2013, p. 64). The Dayton Accords also required the prosecution and termination of police officers and public officials who committed serious offenses against minority rights (Mallinder, 2013). The vetting of security officials took place between 1999 and 2002 by the International Police Task Force (IPTF), created by the UN Security Council in 1995. And lastly, there was judicial vetting between 2002 and 2004. This was conducted by an internationally appointed Independent Judicial Commission (Mallinder, 2013).

However, the vetting process has not gone without its share of criticisms. Some of these shortcomings were addressed in the draft Strategy for Transitional Justice (Kisić, 2013). Kisić (2013) maintains that the prevailing public opinion in Bosnia and Herzegovina is that the institutions that conducted the vetting process were not successful enough and that positions in state institutions are still held by individuals guilty of committing human rights abuses in the past (p. 75). One of the key reasons behind these sentiments is that some certified police officers were later charged and convicted of war crimes (Kisić, 2013, p. 75).

In terms of the judicial side of things, as noted earlier in the introduction chapter, a War Crimes Chamber was established. Although it was established in 2003, this entity did not become operational until 2005. The War Crimes Chamber's objectives are to try cases the ICTY does not manage to process, participate in the reconstruction of the country's judicial system, and play a part in the reconciliation process by bringing war criminals to justice (Van Der Velden, 2010).

In late 2008 the Council of Ministers of Bosnia and Herzegovina adopted the National Strategy for Processing of War Crimes Cases. The strategy devised a systematic approach to processing the large number of war crimes cases in the courts and prosecutor's offices of Bosnia and Herzegovina at both the entity level and the state level (Ministry of Justice Bosnia and Herzegovina, 2008). The strategy details the time frames, capacities, criteria and mechanisms of managing war crimes cases, standardization of court practices, issues of regional cooperation, protection and support to victims and witnesses, as well as financial aspects, and supervision over the implementation of the Strategy (Ministry of Justice Bosnia and Herzegovina, 2008). The document also emphasized the need to process the most complex and highest priority war crimes cases within seven years, and other war crimes cases within 15 years.

As of recently, the war crimes system has been cited as having a severe backlog. War crimes prosecutions even at the highest level have not kept pace with the strategy. According to Džidić (2014), the High Judicial and Prosecutorial Council, the body responsible for supervising Bosnia's justice system, explained that from July 2012 until October 2014, the number of open investigations for war crimes against known suspects decreased from 1,320 to 1,286. The problem of backlog was officially acknowledged in mid-2015 when Bosnia and Herzegovina's Prosecution war crimes department announced that it would not meet its deadline to complete all war crimes cases. The department was still working on 346 of the most complex war crimes cases in relation to 3,383 individuals with estimates of about 500 uncompleted war crimes investigations at the state level and at least as many haven't been completed at the entity level (Human Rights Watch, 2017). There remains talk of revising the National War Crimes Strategy to address a more realistic number of cases within a more realistic time frame.

However, revising the National War Crimes Strategy is all for naught if the key underlining reasons for its demise are not adequately address. Ending the backlog of cases must address the key reasons for the backlog in general. One of the key reasons for the backlog is the poor prioritization the most important cases. Courts at the State, Entity, and local level continue to lack proper coordination, causing some courts to try the same individuals at the same time. Another key issue for the backlog in the Courts of Bosnia and Herzegovina is the lack of trained and professionally competent prosecutorial staff. For instance, the Prosecutor's Office of Bosnia and Herzegovina lacks those with expertise on prosecuting sexual violence crimes. As I noted in chapter three, a key part of implementing transitional justice successfully is for the State allocating the proper human and financial resources. The Prosecutor Office's lack of resources will continue to impede upon prosecuting war times that are of a time sensitive manner, which will further impede upon the strength of the rule of law and respect for legal institutions by Bosnian citizens.

Furthermore, Rangelov and Theros (2007) explain that ethnicity, coupled with nationalism, presents an additional challenge since it was central to the commission of crimes in the conflict and has served to politicize the calls and efforts for justice during the transition. The authors further explain that the Dayton process also contributed to the continued politicization of ethnicity that undermines the process of reconciliation, by entrenching a constitutional structure based on Bosniak, Croat, and Serb 'constituent nations' and effectively mediating political power and participation through ethnic identity. In this context, most developments in transitional justice in Bosnia and Herzegovina have come as a result of pressure from outside forces, most notably the Office of the High Representative (OHR), often by enforcing a compromise on the ethnic elites in charge in the Federation and Republika Srpska, without wide-ranging public consultation or discussion with victims and other civil society groups (Rangelov & Theros, 2007).

Domestic trials too have been fraught with an array of criticism and even attacks by politicians that have sought to undermine the courts and their convictions. In particular, political elites in the Republika Srpska have claimed that war crimes prosecutions have targeted Serbs primarily while allowing war criminals of other ethnic groups escape with impunity. Political elites also continue to publicly support war criminals, deny that genocide took place, and support public events that rally for war criminals. These actions collectively continue to display to the Bosnian public that there is no political will and desire for joint cooperation among its countries, political elites to prosecute war crimes effectively and efficiently so that all victims of 1992-1995 have access to justice.

Moreover, within the last decade, a regional approach to transitional justice, The Coalition for RECOM, has also emerged. The Coalition for RECOM is a non-political regional gathering of civil society organizations. It consists of a network of more than 1900 non-governmental organizations, associations, and individuals who represent and promote the initiative for RECOM toward the establishment of a regional commission tasked with establishing the facts about all victims of war crimes and other serious human rights violations committed in the Territory of the Former Yugoslavia during the period from 1991-2001 (Coalition for RECOM, 2011, p. 3). The coalition for RECOM is outlined in a 30 article statute. While at one point the initiative seemed to have lost its steam as being a feasible mechanism may now be believed to be operational soon. The presidents of Bosnia, Croatia, Montenegro, Serbia, Kosovo, and Macedonia were due to present their joint initiative to the public and to the various national parliaments by the end of January 2015 (Milekić, 2014). However, nothing more has been reported in the press.

Attitudes Towards Transitional Justice and Reconciliation

Perspectives on reconciliation in Bosnia and Herzegovina are no doubt quite complex, as has been demonstrated thus far throughout this book. This part of this chapter explores some attitudes and perspectives on reconciliation as well as how politics in modern Bosnia impacts reconciliation. One of the major recurring questions that emerged throughout this research was the following: do Bosnians even want reconciliation? According to a 2012 survey conducted by Wilkes et al. (2012) in four cities (Banja Luka, Bugojno, Sarajevo, and Mostar), of the 616 respondents, 88.2% affirmed that a process of building trusting and honest relationships would be important for Bosnia and Herzegovina's future. Moreover, 85.4% of the sample believed that such measures would be important for their locality, and 85.6% believed they would be important for the Former Yugoslavia as a whole. The results also demonstrated that trust-building processes that focus on the future received far greater support than those focused on the past, and about half of the respondents reported having found public acknowledgement of past crimes important for public trust in politicians. The survey also noted that there were significant differences among respondents due to their ethnic background.

Interestingly enough, according to Wilkes et al. (2012), the most comparative differences in attitude towards reconciliation did not derive from Croat, Bosniak, and Serb respondents, or respondents from different cities, but responses provided by minorities in those cities. Minorities had less faith in government and public institutions to foster reconciliation. The survey results also found that war time experience impacts attitudes towards reconciliation. For instance, soldiers and civilians attributed greater importance to a reconciliation process than did those who were refugees, or those who answered that they had experienced 'all of the above' or 'none of the above' during the war.

Another interesting factor that this survey examined, which especially concerns this book, was whether or not respondents believed parliament and politicians could foster reconciliation. The results found that there was some divergence across the national communities. Bosniaks placed the most faith in parliament as a site for reconciliation, and Serbs placed the least faith in it. The Bosniak majority in Bugojno placed more faith in the role of politicians in reconciliation at the city level than minorities did. This brings nuance to the data for Bugojno provided above under the section on divergences between respondents living in the four cities selected (Wilkes et al., 2012). There, it was noted that respondents in Bugojno and its vicinity placed less faith in the role of politicians at the city level than at a national level. Also, most strikingly, in Mostar, minority respondents were more likely to credit the role of politicians at the city level than Croats were (Wilkes et al., 2012).

There is also another side to understanding attitude and perspectives on reconciliation, and that is the reality of people understanding what happened and what they are reconciling for. To this day, despite efforts for truth and accountability, there is still no major consensus among the ethnic groups about what happened during the war. Having a collectivized sense of what has taken place fosters responsibility, acknowledgement, and accountability. Kostić (2012) conducted a study in 2005 and 2010 that asked respondents about their views on the role of their own group and the character of the war, as well as to name the defensive military force in the conflict, the results were very interesting. For instance, when asked in 2005 if they agreed with the statement "my people have fought only 'defensive wars,'" an overwhelming majority of Bosniaks (85.3%), Serbs (76.2%), and Croats (75.9%) strongly agreed (Kostić, 2011, p. 655). Although the number of those participants strongly agreeing with the statement fell in 2010, especially among Bosnian Serb population where 54.7% totally agreed, the sentiment that members of their own community fought a defensive war remained consistent across the three ethnicities (Kostić, 2012).

Kostić (2012) also notes that the differences based on ethnic belonging are also rather strong when the respondents are asked to define the character of the war in Bosnia and Herzegovina. He maintains that: it is apparent from the findings that there has been almost no change in the predominant ethno-national definitions of the war in Bosnia and Herzegovina. According to the results of the 2010 survey, 87.4% of Serbs characterized the conflict as a civil war, while 96.6% of Bosniaks and 69.6% of Croats considered it to be an act of aggression on Bosnia and Herzegovina (Kostić, 2011, pp. 655-656).

Lastly, another important aspect to address is how Bosnian attitudes towards reconciliation are impacted in politics. The politics within Bosnia and Herzegovina are just as complicated as their complex multi-layered political system. And these politics are often seen as the main cause for hampering reconciliation. Some journalists and scholars argue that it is nationalist politicians who continue to force nationalist agendas. This can be seen with the general election in October of 2014; according to Latal (2014), after almost four years of political, economic, and social crisis, Bosnians went to the polls weary, as many feared the same ideologies and irresponsible policies would maintain the status quo, or make the situation throughout the country even worse. The author notes that just as in the 1991 election, the 2014 campaign saw hardline Bosnian Serb politicians parading a separatist agenda, some Bosnian Croats still pushing for a separate entity, and Bosniaks arguing for a more centralized state (Latal, 2014).

Others reject these notions. Parish (2012) argues against the sentiments of politicians who enforce ethnic divisions with political agendas in Bosnia and Herzegovina, emphasizing that politicians are feeding off the sentiments and ideologies of the people. He notes that the people of Bosnia and Herzegovina themselves enforce their own ethnic apartheid. Parish (2012) further explains that "on each side of Sarajevo's imperceptible boundary, people watch different television channels, read different newspapers, argue over the merits of different politicians and worship different idols" (para. 14). Parish (2012) also contends: the ethnic divisions in contemporary Bosnia are not, as the international community narrative pretends, the result of intransigent politicians peddling ethno-nationalist agendas. Fear and animosity drive Bosnians' formidable determination not to reintegrate, even when the legal opportunities for them to do so exist. (para. 16)

Regardless of which side is more accurate, Bosnia and Herzegovina still remains a struggling state, and the people are not sure who to blame. Even as Bosnia and Herzegovina battled epic floods along with their neighbors, politics got in the way of memorializing them. Commemoration, unfortunately, became a political battle between politicians in Banja Luka and Sarajevo. The discussions in this section of this chapter make a very strong case for why there must be more research and analysis on the process reconciliation taking in Bosnia and Herzegovina currently.

Conclusion

This chapter laid out the complexities that remain in seeking post-conflict justice in Bosnia and Herzegovina. Regardless of the efforts from the international community and domestic courts, there are many who still are not satisfied. While civil society has played some role in instigating proper discussion on transitional justice and reconciliation. The role has been limited. There are some who use transitional justice as not a means of moving on or as a way to address impunity but as a tool of political fodder. While some of the studies discussed in this chapter note that in some parts of Bosnia and Herzegovina there are those who believe that reconciliation and trust building is necessary to move, while another study posits that all three ethnicities see themselves as having fought a defensive war. Reconciliation or trust building will continue to be hampered as long as there remains competing narratives and victimhoods during the war. But, as noted earlier both reconciliation and transitional justice are elongated processes that could span decades. Twenty three plus years is not enough time to officially say reconciliation is impossible in Bosnia and Herzegovina.

Chapter 7

Transitional Justice Progress in Other Former-Yugoslav States

Jared O. Bell

The previous chapter demonstrates that the international community established tribunals to prosecute war crimes in the former Yugoslav states (Serbia,
Montenegro, Croatia, Bosnia and Herzegovina, and Kosovo). However, what
happened transitional justice processes were utilized in each country where
there was armed conflict? As I noted in chapter three, for transitional justice
measures to flourish, they must be owned by local populations and institutions. This chapter of the book discusses some of these local/domestic transitional justice measures that took in other Yugoslavia states outside of Bosnia
and Herzegovina and the ICTY process.

Croatia

The first country under review is Croatia. Croatia has made some major, positive strides toward dealing with the crimes of the past. Croatia is unique compared to the other states discussed in this section because it is now a European Union (EU) member state. Part of Croatia's criteria in joining the EU was
dealing with its crimes of the past effectively. In terms of domestic trials, Croatia began trials right after the reintegration of territory controlled by rebel
Croatian Serbs at the end of 1996 (Kandić, 2007). At one point, mostly Serbs
had only been tried. The law has provided for trials in absentia. Kandić (2007)
expounds, "[o]bservers from the Organization for Security and Co-Operation
in Europe and from NGOs point to two trials which, according to them, indicate a move forward in relation to the practice to organize trials of Serbs exclusively" (p. 4). For instance, the trial of General Mirko Norac before the
Regional Court in Rijeka for war crimes against Serbian civilians in Gospić
and the renewed trial of officers of the military police for the war crime
against prisoners of war (Serbs) at the military prison Lora indicate a break
with the practice prevailing in Croatia to indict and try Serbs exclusively
(Kandić, 2007). The trial known to the public as the Lora Case, which sought
justice for Serbian victims who were prisoners of war testified for the first
time, contributed to finally getting some recognition for the victims (Kandić,

2007). This participation by Serbian victims resulted in cooperation of the public prosecutor's offices from both Croatia and Serbia (Kandić, 2007). Cruvellier and Valiñas (2006) explain:

> [a]dditionally, in 2004, the Croatian Criminal Code was amended to incorporate the doctrine of command responsibility as a basis of liability, further strengthening the judiciary's power in prosecuting war crimes. Finally, increased interstate judicial cooperation has positively affected investigative efficiency. Nevertheless, significant sources of concern remain: persistent claims of ethnic bias in the proceedings, the conducting of trials in absentia, lack of adequate witness protection, and insufficient legal representation of victims. (p. 2)

Furthermore, in terms of fact finding, independent media sources and NGOs have led truth-seeking initiatives in Croatia (one being RECOM), raising public debate on crimes committed in the past (Cruvellier & Valiñas, 2006). Juxtaposed to these efforts, the Croatian government has made only very limited efforts to expose officially and raise awareness of facts surrounding the crimes committed against non-Croats (Cruvellier & Valiñas, 2006). Despite some of the aforementioned efforts, today there continues to be a systemic denial of any wrongdoing on the part of the Croatian army and of its role in the ethnic cleansing of Serb civilians. The widely accepted narrative instead claims that the war in Croatia was defensive and legitimate, as stated in the "Declaration on the Patriotic War," passed by the parliament in October 2000 (Cruvellier & Valiñas, 2006).

Moreover, in its 2016/2017 annual country report for Croatia, Amnesty International (2016 noted that the ICTY cited major concerns about the pace and effectiveness of prosecutions by the national courts of crimes committed during the 1992-1995 war (para. 5). "The law regulating the status of civilian victims of war passed in 2015 helped ease access to reparations and made it easier for survivors to access crucial services, but challenges remained in providing all victims, especially ethnic minorities, with equal and effective access to justice"(Amnesty International, 2017, para. 5). "Also, for the second consecutive year, no progress was made in establishing the fate and whereabouts of 1,600 persons disappeared during the war"(Amnesty International, 2016, para. 5).

Serbia and Montenegro

The next relevant transitional justice context for discussion is that of Serbia and Montenegro. The union of Serbia and Montenegro took place in 2006, but some of the major developments seen in Serbia or Montenegro came when the two countries were still joined together. Serbia and Montenegro, like Croatia, have made some progress in trying to deal with crimes committed during the conflict across the former Yugoslavia, including Croatia, Bosnia and Herzegovina, and Kosovo. Since the establishment of the Chamber and the Office of the War Crimes Prosecutor in 2003, there has been a slow processing of cases. The progress that has been made was due to the tireless advocacy of civil society groups who pushed for and mobilized a process in which a number of war crimes trials were held in the Belgrade's District Court, including against Serbian citizens for crimes committed across the Serbian border. The work of these civil society groups in providing support to witnesses coming from Croatia, Bosnia, and Kosovo has been crucial to the success of a number of these prosecutions (Tolbert, 2014, para. 3).

In relation to Bosnia and Herzegovina, one of the major complaints from victims has been the large gap in the punishment of war crimes results in punishing perpetrators who committed crimes in Bosnia and Herzegovina. Croats and Serbs alike who committed crimes went to Croatia or Serbia and acquired citizenship and by constitutions or statutes could not be extradited back to Bosnia and Herzegovina to face justice (Documenta, Humanitarian Law Center, & Research and Documentation Center Sarajevo, 2006).

Also, according to Documenta et al. (2006), observers have criticized the Prosecutor's Office for not raising indictments, several years after launching proceedings before the Special Chamber, against highly positioned members of the police and the army for crimes committed by their immediate subordinates. Documenta et al. (2006) also note that a number of legal qualifications in the indictments have caused concern that the prosecutor's office was trying to hide the role played by the state of Serbia in the conflicts on other territories of former Yugoslavia.

Since its independence, other transitional justice efforts in Serbia are primarily the result of vigorous efforts by Serbian civil society groups, such as the Humanitarian Law Center, the Helsinki Committee of Serbia, the Youth Initiative for Human Rights, and others. For example, in Croatia civil society has championed initiatives like the regional commission (RECOM)—a campaign for a regional truth commission to establish facts about all victims of massive crimes committed in the former Yugoslavia between 1991 and 2001 (Tolbert, 2004, para. 3).

Also, when Serbia and Montenegro were still joined together, it was the only country in the region to establish an official truth-telling body. Kandić (2007) note of the commission:

> [t]he decision to set up the truth and reconciliation commission was established on 29 March 2001, with the task of organizing research work to unveil the records concerning the social, inter-communal and political

conflicts which led to war and to cast light on the chain of these events, to keep the domestic and foreign public informed of its work and results; to establish cooperation with related commissions and bodies in the neighboring countries and abroad for the purpose of exchanging their work experience. (p. 6)

The commission ceased in existence in 2003, after the adoption on the 4th of February of the Constitutional Chapter of the State Union of Serbia and Montenegro and the law on its implementation. Not a single report was ever published (Kandić, 2007).

More work needs to be done in Serbia to address the crimes of the past, but another positive step in recent years has been agreements reached between the state prosecutor's offices in Serbia, Croatia, and Bosnia, allowing for cross-border cooperation in the investigation and prosecution of war crimes (Tolbert, 2014, para. 4). Also, in December 2015, the Serbian government unveiled a war crimes strategy that pledged to remedy past failings and prosecute high-level perpetrators who committed large-scale crimes (Ristić, 2015). Along these lines, one major step in a positive direction was in early February 2017 when eight members of a Bosnian Serb special police united were on trial in Belgrade for having a role in the murder of more than 1,300 Bosniak civilians in an agricultural warehouse in the village of Kravica near Srebrenica in July 1995. (Balkans Investigative Reporting Network, 2017, para. 1)

Transitional justice developments in Montenegro alone are another important point to cover. Prosecution and other forms of transitional justice efforts in Montenegro have been rather slow. Only a total of six war crimes cases stemming from the conflicts in the 1990s have been prosecuted in Montenegro's courts. Only three of them have ended in final judgments (Tomović, 2015). The government does have a missing persons commission, which recently agreed to work in cooperation with Kosovo to shed light on the fate of 1,650 people still listed as missing since the end of the Kosovo war (Collaku, 2015).

Kosovo

Kosovo is the youngest state in the former Yugoslavia, having gained its independence from Serbia in 2008. Domestic transitional justice mechanisms are still developing in the nascent country. On August 3, 2015, the Kosovo Parliament passed the "Law on Specialist Chambers and Specialist Prosecutor's Office," a constitutional amendment that establishes a special war crimes court to prosecute former Kosovo Liberation Army (KLA) guerrillas for crimes committed during and after the Kosovo War between January 1, 1998 and December 31, 2000 (International Justice Resource Center, 2015). The court operates under Kosovar law and prosecutes crimes against humanity, war crimes, and organ harvesting, among other crimes. The based in the Netherlands due to concerns regarding judicial corruption and the lack of a substantial witness protection program in Kosovo (International Justice Review Center, 2015). Also, on February 13, 2017 President Hashim Thaci announced the creation of a Truth Commission aimed at reconciling relations Kosovo's ethnic-Albanian majority and Serb minorities and to find answers for alleged atrocities committed during the 1998-99 Kosovo war (Bytyci, 2017).

Conclusion

One of the key reasons I added this chapter, was because I felt that gauging what was going on in the region as it related to domestic transitional justice and not just Bosnia and Herzegovina was important. Transitional justice processes in other Former Yugoslav States have made some positive strides toward addressing crimes from the wars in the 1990s, but like Bosnia and Herzegovina there remains a lot of work that must be done to combat impunity and address the needs of victims. One relative aspect that we can see in each case is that progress seems to hinge on political will. The issue of addressing post-conflict justice remains a resounding discussion in the Western Balkans region in general. In September of 2016, I attended a forum in Sarajevo organized by the Balkans Investigative Reporting Network and one of the key elements of transitional justice that was discussed is the lack of political will to address the war crimes and that includes harmonizing laws, resources, and funding across the region. Perhaps, regional war crimes and Transitional Justice Strategy are needed now that the ICTY is defunct. However, this will require a lot of concessions on all states involved, which would depend upon navigating a mountain of ethnic politics and sentiments.

Chapter 8

Methodological Considerations

Jared O. Bell

To reiterate, the purpose of this research was to explore whether or not Bosnians believe that the National Transitional Justice Strategy and its proposed mechanisms would be effective in fostering perspectives of reconciliation. There has been a lot of research on transitional justice, but very few investigations have actually focused on non-judicial transitional justice mechanisms. As noted in the introduction, transitional justice mechanisms again are essentially public policies, and public policies created in parliaments or legislatures do not always meet the needs, expectations, or have the faith, will, and trust of the people. This is where this research contributes to scholarship and literature on transitional justice because there has been no major study that explores the proposed Transitional Justice Strategy in Bosnia and Herzegovina from the perspectives of everyday Bosnians.

This research aims to not only contribute transitional justice research but also to the body of literature on challenges post-conflict societies face in general. The more that is known about how reconciliation relates to certain mechanisms, the more professionals in the field can enhance them. I argue that more people-centered approaches are necessary to measure and employ transitional justice mechanisms that are not so very technical, that bridge theory and practice, and that consider the expectations of the people who the mechanisms are aimed at helping. This research explored these concepts further and perhaps will serve as a starting point for others who intend to explore this topic, which then may expand the literature on this subject even further. Chapman (2009) reminds the audience that carefully designed empirical research can play a major role in helping theorists and practitioners better understand the requirements of national reconciliation, as well as provide tools for gauging progress and identifying problems in a given society.

Study Setting

This study took place online and surveyed residents in three cities in Bosnia and Herzegovina. The cities were Sarajevo, Mostar, and Banja Luka. While there are other cities that could have been used, I chose these three cities were because they are a) three of the largest cities in Bosnia and Herzegovina, and are b) comprised of different ethnic and religious groups and therefore, represent large cross-sections of the Bosnian population. Sarajevo hosts a mixed population but is largely comprised of Bosniak who make up 77.4% of the city; Banja Luka is largely Serb and Orthodox with Serbs over 54% of the city, and Mostar is largely Croat and Catholic accounting for 53.9% of the city. The sample totaled 487 respondents: 186 from Sarajevo, 120 from Mostar, and 167 from Banja Luka. I did not want to choose cities that were predominately Bosniak, Serb, or Croat; had I done that, there would not have been enough diversity for comparison. These two reasons point to the main fact that I wanted to be able to make sure I got enough of diversity from each ethnic group.

Data Collection Procedures

Data collection was done through a single online quantitative survey. The survey was administered through SurveyMonkey (www.surveymonkey.com). A Facebook page dedicated to this study was created; I marketed and shared the survey through this social media platform. Through Facebook, I was able to determine my target population and sampling for the survey. The survey was also shared through an online discussion forum (www.hercegbosna .org/forum/). Participants were recruited using the recruitment statement letter in Appendix A (English) and and Appendix B (Serbo-Croatian). On both Facebook and the discussion forum, the survey was shared with the recruitment statement prefacing the actual survey link.

Using a quantitative survey allowed me to measure attitudes more effectively and inexpensively, and the process was not very time-consuming. Chapman (2009) explains that surveys based on random selection and population-based sampling have the advantage of enabling researchers to draw conclusions about the attitudes of a large and diverse population from a relatively small sample size. In this study, the instrument was used to measure four independent variables and one dependent variable. These are outlined below:

Independent Variable – Ethnicity, Age, Gender, City Location

Dependent Variable – Perceptions of Reconciliation.

Lastly, the data in this study was collected in an ethical manner. It was understood that some of the survey participants might be considered members of vulnerable populations. A vulnerable population in the context of this study refers to those who may have been victims, or family members may have been victims of violence or trauma. Of course, there would be no way for me as the researcher to determine vulnerability across the board from an online survey.

So, the questions on the survey were designed carefully so as not to be very intrusive or have possible victims relive traumas of the conflict. Of course, this can never be avoided in any study 100%. This survey was administered freely without coercion, and the full intentions for the collection of data were explained in the survey's letter of participation. The surveys were collected in an anonymous fashion, and the participants were made aware of this method. Consent was sought through an online participation letter through which participants were informed of the study and their right to participate or not to participate. Those who wanted to participate did so by clicking "yes" at the bottom of the participation letter which then took them forward to the actual survey.

Instrument

The survey consisted of a 13 question survey. The context of the survey was developed based on the review of literature discussed above. The survey was designed to bridge gaps between what is already discussed about transitional justice mechanisms and reconciliation in Bosnia and Herzegovina and what remains unknown. As it was noted in chapter six that Bosnians see reconciliation as an important part of countering their past. The survey used in this study was designed to explore whether or not a government led solution can foster this reconciliation. It is important to note that internet respondents are usually quite different from real-time respondents in the fact that they have access to a variety of sources on certain topics and are more than likely to have different opinions than those who do not. (Please see the participation letters in Appendixes A and B. Survey A is in English (Appendix E) and Survey B is in Serbo-Croatian (Appendix F). Survey results for each question appear in the following chapter. The survey questions and their rationale are explained below as follows:

1. **Are you familiar with the proposed Transitional Justice Strategy?** This question was designed to yield information on how informed members of the general Bosnian populace are on the issue.

2. **If so how did you learn about it?** This question was designed to yield information about how well the draft Transitional Justice Strategy has been introduced to the general public.

3. **The strategy focuses on five key areas for addressing the conflict in the 1990s: truth and fact finding, reparations, rehabilitation, memorialization, and institutional reform. Do you think these areas address the main issues blocking reconciliation?** This question was designed to yield information that tells if these key

areas address the concerns of members of the general Bosnian population, hence also telling whether or not the strategy will be effective or not.

4. **Do you think the above processes are needed for Bosnia and Herzegovina to move forward from its past?** This question was designed to gauge the perspectives of members of the general Bosnian populace on whether or not the processes are important to move forward. The responses to this question yielded information that tells whether or not any of the above mechanisms are needed, hence also telling how relevant and successful the Transitional Justice Strategy will be.

5. **What of the five processes do you think is the most important out of the five key areas mention in question for reconciliation to take place in Bosnia and Herzegovina? Check more than one if it applies.** This question was designed to yield information that tells how valued one of the key areas may be over another.

6. **Do you think reconciliation in Bosnia and Herzegovina is possible period?** This questioned was designed to yield information that helps determine if reconciliation is possible from the perspectives of Bosnians regardless of the method or strategy employed.

7. **If you believe reconciliation is possible, do you have faith in the Bosnian government to lead the efforts of reconciliation?** This question was designed to yield information as to whether or not respondents believe the government can lead reconciliation efforts regardless of the strategy or mechanisms.

8. **Will activities in these key areas impact you or your family personally? If yes, which ones? Check more than one if more than one applies.** This question was designed to inquire how immediately relevant these key areas are to the lives of the respondents. The responses to this question also yielded information that shows how people impacted by the proposed strategy may respond versus those who are not impacted.

9. **Will participating in any of the above activities or receiving any of benefits help you personally be able to reconcile the past and move on?** This question was designed to inquire if receiving ben-

efits or compensation for past wrongs impact their perceptions on reconciliation.

10. **Which city do you live in?** This question was designed to find out demographic information about the respondents. The responses to this question yielded information about variances in responses of the residents from different cities, which allowed for comparison of how location may impact people's perspectives and hence their responses.

11. **What ethnicity do you consider yourself?** This question was designed to find out demographic information about the respondents. The responses to this question yielded information about variances in responses from different ethnicities, which allowed for comparisons on how ethnicity may impact some people's perspectives and hence their responses.

12. **What is your gender?** This question was designed to find out demographic information about the respondents. The responses this question yielded information about variances in responses from different genders, which allowed for comparison of how gender may impact their perspectives and hence their responses.

13. **What is your age range?** This question was designed to find out demographic information about the respondents. The responses to this question yielded information about variances in responses of different ages, which allowed for comparison of how age may impact people's perspectives and hence their responses.

Having discussed the questions that were used in the survey and their purpose in relation to this study, the population and the sample that was used are explored next.

Population and Sampling Plan

The original survey sample size was set at 450 respondents. This sample population size was chosen by adding the population of Sarajevo, Banja Luka, and Mostar which totals a population of 681,894. When using a confidence level of 99% and a confidence interval of 0.06076 a sample size of 450 is yielded. This configuration was done by using a sample calculator at http://www.nss.gov.au/ nss/home.nsf/pages /Sample+size+ calculator. However, 487 responses were collected. The responses were not collected in equal numbers due to each city's different population density. Sarajevo proper is home to about 369,534 residents, Banja Luka 199,191 residents, and Mostar 113,169 residents. Getting respondents in Mostar was more difficult than getting respondents in Sarajevo or Banja Luka. I would say that this has to do with the population density, and also when using Facebook marketing, there are more keywords for Sarajevo and Banja Luka and Sarajevo than there are for Mostar. So, more people in these larger cities, of course, had more access than those in Mostar. Rather than reconfigure a new lower sample size so the number of respondents would be equal across all cities, all data was used as it was collected. Lowering sample size would have misrepresented Mostar's true data collection percentage. Furthermore, the survey was active on Survey-Monkey for two months from early June to early August of 2015.

The sampling was a random non-probability methodology. The targeted respondents were residents of the three cities discussed above ranging in ages from 18 to 65. The participation age range was set at 18, because it is highly unlikely that people below the age of 18 would have any in-depth knowledge of the war, justice processes, national politics, etc. While I could not find a recent breakdown of each city's age and gender demographics, looking at the overall demographics gives a general picture of how the country is broken down. The overall age and breakdown of sex and age across Bosnia and Herzegovina are: 0-14 years: 13.7% (male 272,812/female 256,152), 15-24 years: 12.7% (male 255,074/female 238,428), 25-54 years: 46.6% (male 906,265 /female 899,870), 55-64 years: 13.7% (male 253,045/female 276,769), 65 years and over: 13.3% (male 199,515/female 313,713).

Data Analysis Strategy

Four types of analysis were used for the hypothesis testing. The statistical analysis software used was SPSS. The four tests I used in this section were the Chi-Square tests. This test was selected because a Chi-Square test is used to best determine whether there is a significant association between two or more variables, and all four hypotheses are designed to measure associations between two or more variables. Chi-Square tests are popular for both social and scientific research.

The specific hypotheses to be tested are shown below in null form:

1. (Null) H_0: There will be no association between belief in the effectiveness of the Transitional Justice Strategy and belief that the Bosnian government's efforts will lead to reconciliation.

(Alternative) H_A: There will be association between belief in the effectiveness of the Transitional Justice Strategy and belief that the Bosnian government's efforts will lead to reconciliation.

This test analyzed responses from these two questions: The strategy focuses on five key areas for addressing the conflict in the 1990s: truth and fact finding, reparations, rehabilitation, memorialization, and institutional reform. Do you think that these areas address the main issues that have stopped Bosnia and Herzegovina from moving on? If you believe moving on is possible, do you have faith in the Bosnian government to lead the efforts to move on? The data analyzed in this test one were nominal. The questions were both yes or no questions. And yes or no questions have no intrinsic value ordered to the categories.

2. (Null) H_0: There will be no statistically significant difference in the perspectives on whether it is possible for Bosnia and Herzegovina to move on between Bosniaks and Croats, and Serbs.

    (Alternative) H_A: Bosniaks and Croats will be more likely to believe that it is possible for Bosnia and Herzegovina to move on than Serbs.

    This test analyzed how participants of different ethnicities have responded to this one question: The strategy focuses on five key areas for addressing the conflict in the 1990s: truth and fact finding, reparations, rehabilitation, memorialization, and institutional reform. Do you think these areas address the main issues that have stopped Bosnia and Herzegovina from moving on? The data analyzed in this test were nominal because neither question had an intrinsic value ordered to either category.

3. (Null) H_0: There will be no statistically significant difference in the belief that the government of Bosnia and Herzegovina can lead efforts towards reconciliation between respondents between the ages of 18 and 33 and respondents between the ages of 55 and 65.

    (Alternative) HA: Respondents between the ages of 18 and 33 will be more likely to believe that the government of Bosnia and Herzegovina can lead efforts towards reconciliation than respondents between the ages of 55 and 65.

This test analyzed how participants from the different locations have responded to this one question: If you believe moving on is possible, do you have faith in the Bosnian government to lead the efforts to move on? The data analyzed in this test were nominal. One question queries about the age of respondents and the other question is a yes or no question. Neither has an intrinsic value ordered to it.

4.   (Null) H_0: There will be no difference in belief between men and women that the drafts Transitional Justice Strategy's five key areas will be adequate in helping Bosnia and Herzegovina address its issues.

(Alternative) H_A: Male respondents will be more likely to believe that the draft Transitional Justice Strategy's five key areas will be adequate in helping Bosnia and Herzegovina address its issues.

This test analyzed how participants of different genders have responded to this one question: The strategy focuses on five key areas for addressing the conflict in the 1990s: truth and fact finding, reparations, rehabilitation, demoralization, and institutional reform. Do you think these areas address the main issues that have stopped Bosnia and Herzegovina from moving on? The data analyzed in this test were nominal. One question inquires about the gender of the respondents, and the other question is a yes or no question. Neither have an intrinsic value ordered to them. All hypotheses were tested at a minimum of the .05 level of significance.

Conclusion

This chapter essentially lays the foundation for this entire research project. While the historical background, theory, and topical literature discussed in the previous chapters are all important in understanding why this project was designed and gives some context as to where it fits with current scholarship on the topics of transitional justice in Bosnia and Herzegovina, this chapter actually shows how the study was calibrated and where the results and discussion chapters have their roots. One particularly neat aspect of this research design is that it utilizes social media, which is a nuanced way of doing social science research, especially as it relates to transitional justice. Studying a particular social phenomenon is not easy, there are always limitations to gaining access to participants.

However, social media opens up a whole new door that would have been closed before. No longer do we have to always be in a village, town, city, or country to collect major data that can be used in academic research or policy making. Now that the project has been completed I realized also that I might have explored and asked other questions beyond the 13 that I did ask. After I read over the data collected, I realized I wanted to know about thoughts on how the general population of Bosnia felt about this strategy as a means of local ownership compared to that of the ICTY. I believe gauging general knowledge about local transitional justice processes from participants could have also been informative. However, at the same time, I did not want to create a very long, drawn-out survey that would have discouraged participants from voicing their opinions.

Chapter 9

Findings and Implications

Jared O. Bell

Chapter nine discusses the findings from each question, the hypothetical tests, and their implications as to whether or not the Transitional Justice Strategy will foster reconciliation from the perspectives of everyday Bosnians. However, before moving to discuss each question and the hypotheses, I would like to discuss some of the background research I did while in Bosnia from late April to mid-May of 2015. Also, it is important to discuss the time period during which the survey data was collected. I believe this information will provide additional context for understanding the perspectives of the Transitional Justice Strategy besides those that were discussed in chapters one and six.

While conducting field research in Sarajevo, the capital of Bosnia and Herzegovina, I was able to meet with representatives from the Post-Conflict Research Center and the Balkans Investigative Reporting Network in Sarajevo, as well as one of the members of the expert working group who was responsible for drafting the Transitional Justice Strategy. Much of what they discussed with me seemed to be connected and mirrored a lot of the key issues discussed throughout the earlier chapters in this book. One of the overarching themes I took from these meetings was that Bosnia and Herzegovina still struggles with the issue of establishing a collective truth. There are still no largely established facts outside of the fact that 100,000 people were killed during the war. What happened, the extent of what happened, and who is responsible still remains a largely, furiously debated topic. The aforementioned study conducted in 2005 and 2010 discussed in chapter six that discusses attitudes towards reconciliation in Bosnia and Herzegovina, Kostić (2012) cites that the majority of people belonging to different ethnic groups believed their group fought defensively in the war between 1992-1995. Five years after his study, sentiments on what seems to be the truth largely remain the same. Apparently, even members of the expert working group struggled to define an appropriate truth-telling mechanism, as the section that discusses this in the strategy is quite vague.

Another major theme I took from the meetings that also mirrors what was discussed in both chapters one and three and is that the political and financial support for this strategy and transitional justice mechanisms in Bosnia and Herzegovina still remains elusive. What is more, there seems to be very little political will to act on passing any real measures of the strategy. As noted earlier in chapter one, the Republika of Srpska stopped sending representatives to the meetings altogether as they feared losing some level of autonomy from the process. I also learned that there was very little promotion of the strategy by the working group or any government office for people to learn about the strategy and how it may actually impact their lives. None of the three experts I met with believed that this strategy would ever come to fruition, at least not in its entirety. One of the main examples that came up from one of these meetings was the implementation of the war crimes strategy and the fact that while it exists, very little of it has been implemented as it is designed on paper and it still lacks many of the resources and coordination needed to make prosecution effective and less backlogged. This speaks to another important theme along these lines that also came up during each meeting, and that is that there is no problem with civil society and government in Bosnia and Herzegovina recognizing problems or identifying issues, and what the solutions to those issues maybe, but when it comes to actual implementation there is little to no coordination or follow through in fixing them. I would argue that this is perhaps attributed to the political culture of Bosnia and Herzegovina.

The political culture in Bosnia and Herzegovina is still developing. Bosnians are now solely responsible for their own government and societal changes. As noted above in chapters one and two, Bosnia and Herzegovina has historically had a long history of foreign occupation or involvement in a socialist federal system. And since the end of the war, Bosnia and Herzegovina until very recently has been administered and financed by the international community. Bosnians are now grappling with how to make their institutions run and be efficient without some foreign power and influence forcing them to do so. Many scholars posit that apathy exists when it comes to making political changes in Bosnia and Herzegovina. Banović (2016) notes that the citizens of Bosnia and Herzegovina "are aware of their political rights and express the need to participate in the public sphere, but in practical terms, the political behavior of citizens is characterized by apathy and indolence in relation to politics" (p. 6). This apathy and indolence can be attributed to why many policies fail to be implemented in Bosnia and Herzegovina.

Moving on, it is also important to discuss the socio-political context and background of when the surveys were conducted. I'm not claiming that the results were necessarily impacted by these events, but I think it's important to consider national discourse that was taking place while people were responding on sensitive issues related to what was happening then in real time. July 11, 2015, marked the 20th anniversary of the genocide at Srebrenica. Using the term genocide to describe what happened in Srebrenica has been very controversial and divisive in Bosnia and Herzegovina, Serbia, and throughout the entire world. A UN Security Council Resolution commemorating the massacre was vetoed by Russia for using semantics that seemed too anti-Serb. The killings of Srebrenica are like the rest of the war, still largely contested between those who argue that what happened was systematic and therefore equate it to genocide versus those who say it was not systematic and designed to eliminate Muslims in the eastern part of Bosnia and Herzegovina and that the bloodshed was just a factor in the war.

Another divisive event that took place during the data collection period from June to August 2015 in Bosnia and Herzegovina occurred when Republika of Srpska's President Milorad Dodik pushed for a referendum on the legitimacy of Bosnia's national court, arguing that the court was largely biased against Bosnian Serbs when it came to war crimes prosecutions and argued that many Bosniaks have not been charged at the same rate. This incident drew large criticism and disapproval from the international community as it was viewed as an affront to the country's Dayton-designed constitution and had the potential to destabilize Bosnia and Herzegovina as a whole and possibly the entire region.

General Survey Findings

I will now move on to discuss and analyze the results from each question and hypothetical test. Where appropriate some of the findings from the general survey are also compared and contrasted with other research studies on Bosnia and Herzegovina, as well as other transitional justice context from across the globe. While this study is unique, I believe exploring these other studies and their findings, in contrast to my own, will allow for an interesting and more robust perspective that can confirm the validity of the findings of this study. I also believe that contrasting and comparing different research studies and contexts allows for one to see and understand key themes and challenges in the transitional justice field in general and not just within a specific country or region.

Based on the data in Figure 1, it becomes apparent that the majority of respondents at 57.38% have not heard of the Bosnian Government's proposed Transitional Justice Strategy compared to the 42.62% who have. This shows that the majority of respondents knew nothing about the strategy before taking the survey. This also may call into consideration the results for responses to the other questions. The more knowledge someone has on a particular topic, the more he or she will be able to have more of a concrete opinion or idea. Perhaps if more people knew about the Strategy before taking the survey, the results may have been entirely different. This question was not one of the main ones used to run the hypothetical tests, but it is still an important one.

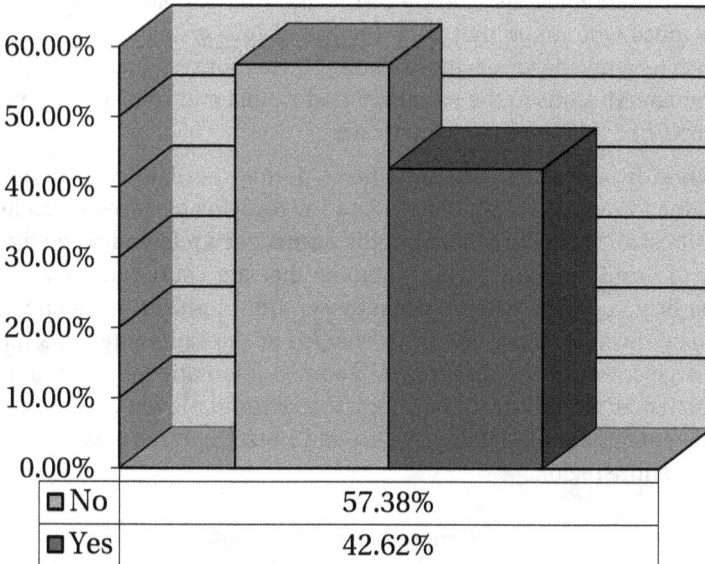

▫ No	57.38%
▪ Yes	42.62%

Figure 1. Summary of responses to survey question 1: Are you familiar with the National Transitional Justice Strategy?

The main objective of this research project was to gauge perspectives on the Transitional Justice Strategy and reconciliation, and it would be impossible to fully do this without knowing how many people actually were familiar with the Strategy itself. I argue that this is parallel to what was discussed earlier. Since there was not much attention or marketing of the Strategy for the general public, very few people had actually heard of or learned about the Strategy. The five consultations held were not enough to gauge all of the public. I argue that perhaps consultations should have been increased in quantity and length. Office of the United Nations Commissioner for Human Rights (2009) maintains that "more drawn-out consultations may facilitate acceptance of the process on the part of consultees, a maturation of their viewpoints and an ongoing refinement of methodologies" (p. 17). The Office also notes that South Africa deliberately avoided a rushed consultation process. The preparatory activities for the Truth and Reconciliation Commission happened over an 18-month period following democratic elections in 1994 (UNOHCHR, 2009).

As noted in chapter one, the strategy invited a host of civil society actors from across Bosnia and Herzegovina to take part in the designing of the strategy. But, we must honestly consider how much weight civil society pulls in everyday Bosnian society. As I noted earlier in chapter six, while civil society in Bosnia and Herzegovina has been an active participant addressing the past, their impact has been relatively limited, so using civil society as the main means of disseminating information to or engaging the general public, was one of the flaws of this strategies design. The UNDP-BiH's (United Nations Development Program in Bosnia and Herzegovina) (2011) special report "Facing the Past and Access to Justice from a Public Perspective", found that 64.9% of the 1,600 participants from across Bosnia and Herzegovina, including the Federation of Bosnia and Herzegovina, the Republika Srpska, and the Brčko District were not aware of the activities of a large number of NGOs that were doing work in collecting documents, accounts, and testimonies about the past war, compared to the 35.1% who were (p. 24). These numbers show that civil society organizations are not informing the general public in Bosnia and Herzegovina of their own transitional justice activities, let alone activities happening at the state level.

Interestingly enough, I believe a good example we can explore in relation to outreach and transitional justice is the outreach strategy executed by the International Criminal Court (ICC) in the Central African Republic. To address concerns of the local community, the Court's outreach program was created to: "(1) provide accurate and comprehensive information to affected communities regarding the Court's role and activities; (2) promote greater understanding of the Court's role during the various stages of proceedings with a view to increasing support for them among the population; (3) foster greater participation of local communities in the activities of the Court; (4) respond to the general concerns and expectations expressed by affected communities and by particular groups within these communities; (5) counter misinformation; and (6) promote access to, and understanding of, judicial proceedings among affected communities" (Vinck and Pham, 2010, p. 4). The court primarily used mass media as the main of reaching the general public. The results from the population based study conducted by Vinck and Pham (2010) found that this has been an effective way to raise awareness and increase knowledge about the court.

Vinck and Pham (2010) also found in their research that increased knowledge of the ICC was associated with positive perceptions and attitudes toward the Court. For instance, they note that among those who had heard about the ICC in the general population survey, nearly all "(95%) believed the ICC to be important, citing in another more open-ended question that it would answer the need for justice (51%), punish those responsible (20%) or compensate victims (10%). Respondents associated the ICC with bringing justice (27%), helping prevent future crimes (20%), helping establish the truth about what happened (19%), punishing those responsible (14%), helping victims (9%) and bringing peace (8%)" (p. 35). This case illustrates the importance and how beneficial outreach can be in terms of shaping perceptions around transitional justice mechanisms.

This case also illustrates that keeping the general public informed also helps them to understand some of the core purposes and notions of transitional justice mechanisms. Which has not been the case in Bosnia and Herzegovina. I believe that many everyday Bosnians do not particularly understand the concept of transitional justice and what it means beyond the retributive sense that many have seen played out at the ICTY and domestic courts.

Also, to revert back to what I noted in chapter six again, since there have been many failed attempts at developing comprehensive transitional justice mechanisms in Bosnia and Herzegovina, I argue that many people are seemingly weary to pay attention or invest their hopes in yet another proposed transitional justice feat just to have their hopes dashed and disappointed again. I also argue that the complexities of transitional justice and the lack of concrete public education and information has also caused this fatigue. Meaning it is easy for some members of the general population to get tired of hearing about transitional justice processes if they do not see the central value to their daily lives and their struggles. However, I believe civil society could be a major game changer in this regard, as I noted in chapter three civil societies can play an implicit role in helping to grow more public support, as well as spur public interest and engagement in implementing the transitional in the strategy.

The most pressing issue concerning civil society organizations in Bosnia and Herzegovina is that, as noted earlier in chapter six, many of their efforts remain uncoordinated, so there are very few united fronts trying to engage people. The State should also be working to empower civil society and recognize their role in aiding the State in the ongoing transitional justice processes that are taking place, none of which is happening in Bosnia and Herzegovina currently. While the draft Transitional Justice Strategy calls for it, there is no call for a united and coherent outreach plan to reach all citizens of Bosnia and Herzegovina on the issue. This is particularly unfortunate, because many Bosnians believe an actual Transitional Justice Strategy is actually needed. According to data from the previously mentioned UNDP-BiH's (2011) special report, when respondents were asked the questions, "To what extent do you agree or disagree with the following statement: The authorities in BIH should devise a concrete plan for facing the past and truth-seeking issues?", the vast majority of the respondents (nearly 90%) gave a positive answer.

No matter if this Strategy ever comes to be a reality or not, any other transitional justice mechanisms that may develop in Bosnia and Herzegovina outreach will have to be a must. The absence of an active outreach programme and engagement with the press and public in the early years allowed politicians and local media to fill the void and shape the discourse with misinformation and criticisms. As noted earlier, this is particularly happening with the domestic war crimes trials currently in Bosnia and Herzegovina. They are subject to interpretation by political elites, who operate for their own benefit and not necessarily for the benefit of the country. These attacks on the courts have also weakened its legitimacy, and while there have been some attempts to rebuff this, a lot of the damage already been done (Haider, 2016). Now both state institutions and civil society must work to counter this damage effectively and show that some progress has been made towards post-conflict justice, and the only real way is to inform the general public and engage it concretely.

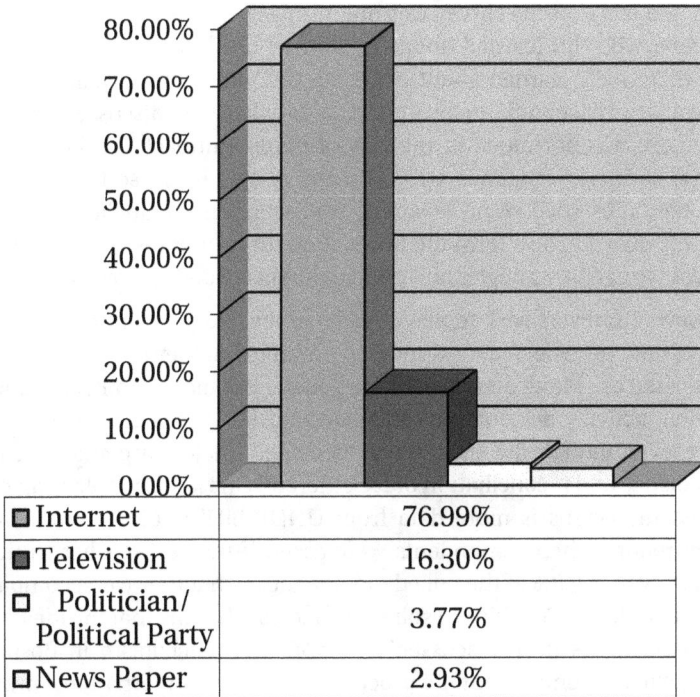

■ Internet	76.99%
■ Television	16.30%
□ Politician/ Political Party	3.77%
□ News Paper	2.93%

Figure 2. Summary of responses to survey question 2: If so how did you hear about it?

The data in this graph demonstrates that the majority of respondents learned about the strategy, firstly through the Internet at 76.99%, secondly through television at 16.32%, thirdly through politicians or political at 3.77%, and lastly through newspapers at 2.93%. These statistics are not surprising considering that the survey was on the internet. Nevertheless, finding out how people learned of the strategy is important because one can see how the strategy may have been marketed. Understanding how the strategy may have been marketed provides more insight into how people may have come to perceive it, and therefore how they responded to the survey questions distributed for this study. For instance, if someone learned about the strategy over the internet, he or she probably did his or her own research and formed his or her own opinions based on that research. However, if people heard about it from a political party, they may have gotten information that was biased based on that political party's leanings. However, the fact only 2.93% only heard about the strategy from political parties, also may mean that politicians may not have even been vested enough to discuss the Strategy openly within the public sphere and their constituents.

Also, the fact that the survey was online speaks to the fact that the majority of people who did learned about it, learned about it online. Many people more than likely learned about it for the first time after clicking the advertisements on Facebook. Referring again to what was discussed previously, since there was not much in the way of public outreach on the strategy or political support, explaining why so many people heard so little about it in other mediums such as newspapers, television, and politicians. The results from this question also form the foundation for further research into the best avenues to market strategies and policies in Bosnia and Herzegovina.

However, to revert back to what I said earlier in this chapter everyday Bosnians cannot be expected to support something that they are not familiar with or educated on. Many members of the general population in Bosnia and Herzegovina, actually are not even familiar with key terms around transitional justice, even though the country has become a major case study for transitional justice and reconciliation or lack thereof. One key example I can offer to buttress my claims is more data from UNDP-BiH's (2011) aforementioned special report, when respondents were asked if they knew what truth commissions were, 60.8% of the polled did not know what they were, compared to 37.2% that did (p. 25). This is a sobering fact, considering that the idea of truth commissions has been discussed as a potential mechanism in Bosnia and Herzegovina to compliment the process domestic and international processes that took place in The Hague.

Moreover, what is particularly unique about this study and I believe where this research makes a big difference is that while collecting data, it also educated people on a major transitional justice process. I argue that this could have been a major way for the government and other stakeholders interested in implementing the strategy to educate people and to draw the support of the public. Kastner (2013) argues that new technologies (such as the internet) may play an important role in increasing access to transitional justice institutions and in facilitating communication between the institutions and their constituencies (p. 9) He notes that "ideally, this technology can be used to increase the flow of information in a unidirectional manner, i.e., from the institution to the local communities, but to facilitate dialogical communication" (p. 9).

This is would not be a new practice in Bosnia and Herzegovina entirely, for instance, the High Judicial and Prosecutorial Council of Bosnia and Herzegovina initiated an information campaign in 2006, for the purpose of providing information to the general public about its role institution, as well as the processes of judicial reform (Hrlović, 2013, p. 48). I believe the internet could have been and can still be used an efficient way to engage people across Bosnia and Herzegovina as it relates to educating and engaging citizens on issues of transitional justice. According to the International Telecommunications Union (2017), 77.5% of Bosnian households possess a computer, while 61.5% of the population had Internet access at home. Not to mention that there is also internet available at a number of cafes, public squares, restaurants, etc. These statistics show very well that the internet can be a place that can be used to engage individuals on key social issues like transitional justice. In many regards, social media outlets like Twitter and Facebook play a major role in social and political organizing in Bosnia and Herzegovina (Global Information Society Watch, 2011). "Facebook, and recently Twitter and Google+, are considered a public sphere where the majority of people connect and where activists can promote their causes and reach the support of critical masses"(GISW, 2011, p. 89). As I discussed earlier, I used Facebook to market my surveys, on the public page I created for its marketing, some participants choose to have discussion and dialog about the survey, transitional justice, war crimes, etc. Besides Facebook, there are other ways to now have online dialogs such as the Convetit platform or Moodle, which allows users to participate in an active online forum. I believe such online platforms can revolutionize transitional justice outreach and general societal engagement. This outreach and engagement can and will definitely have an impact on helping local populations take ownership more effectively in transitional justice processes.

The data in Figure 3 demonstrates that the majority of respondents at 50.94% felt that the five key areas addressed the main issues that have stopped Bosnia and Herzegovina from moving compared to those who think it will not at 49.06%. The findings of this question are important because they point to the crux of this research. This finding implies that the majority felt that the key areas in this strategy have potential to foster reconciliation. So here, part of the answer to the overall question arises. This will also have an impact on other survey questions as well; for instance, if respondents felt that the strategy and its five areas are adequate to move the country forward, then they would have been more likely to feel that participating in mechanisms of these key areas would have helped them to move on personally.

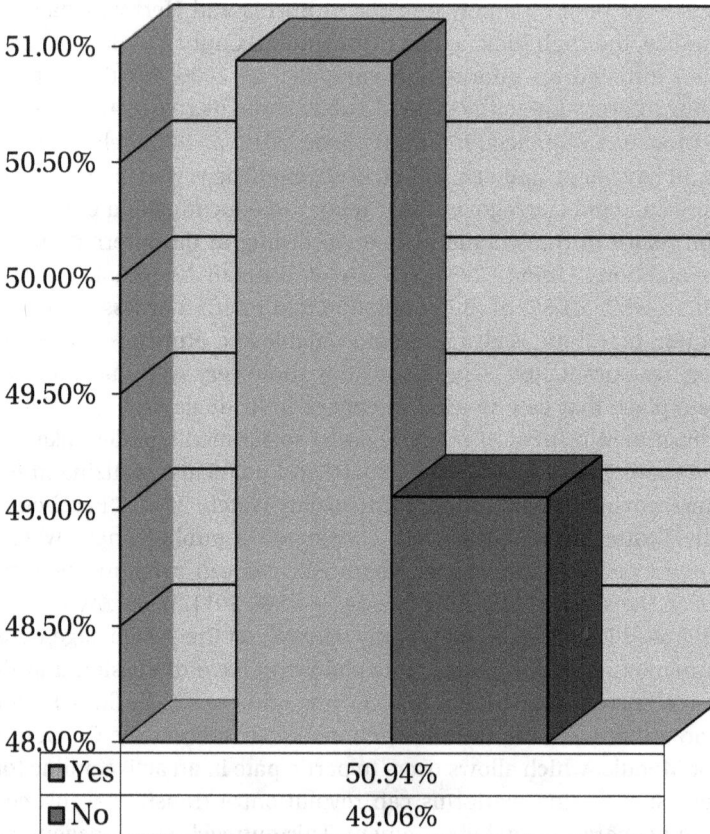

▣ Yes	50.94%
▣ No	49.06%

Figure 3. Summary of responses to survey question 3: The strategy focuses on five key areas for addressing the conflict in the 1990s, truth and fact finding, reparations, rehabilitation, memorialization, and institutional reform. Do you think these areas address the main issues blocking reconciliation?

The aforementioned Special Report commissioned by UNDP-BiH also explored this notion and I have recognized similar themes from their findings in relation to my own as it relates to the Transitional Justice Strategy. For instance, the study asked the question: "BiH Committed itself to a plan, i.e., a BiH Transitional Justice Strategy, and a concrete action plan for its implementation. What in your opinion should be the main goal of this strategy"? 29.9% of respondents said that ensuring justice for the victims was a top priority, while 27% wanted the strategy to focus on building and encouraging dialog about the war. Meanwhile, 23.0% of respondents said that divising activities related to seeking the truth about the war in Bosnia and Herzegovina. Followed by 9.2% wanted the State to clearly define the issue of reparations for war victims, and then 6.1% of respondents who wanted to develop a more concrete vetting system for public officials (UNDP-BiH, 2011, p. 21).

I believe these results show that Bosnians particularly want a transitional justice process beyond the ICTY and domestic courts. As noted in earlier chapters, a lot of emphasis has been put on retributive justice in the Bosnian context that has not necessarily fostered reconciliation or healing. Especially as it relates to extracting the truth. Which seems to be a continuous theme in Bosnia and Herzegovina's transitional justice context. Orlović (2013) explains that despite various court rulings, a large number of Bosnia and Herzegovina's citizens still believe that facts about the 1992-1995 war have yet to be concretely established. As I discussed earlier one mechanism or approach to justice cannot reconcile the past alone or foster new relations. According to the United Nations Secretary General's Note on Transitional Justice Approaches (2010) "Effective transitional justice programmes utilize coherent and comprehensive approaches that integrate the full range of judicial and non-judicial processes and measures, including truth-seeking, prosecution initiatives, reparations programmes, institutional reform including vetting processes, or an appropriately conceived combination thereof" (p. 6). I believe these set of proposed mechanism offered a combination that put more emphasis on fostering reconciliation about the past and it was a process that was particularly designed with the input of actors in Bosnian society.

The data in Figure 4 shows that the majority of respondents at 74.90% felt that the above processes (truth and fact finding, reparations, rehabilitation, memorialization, and institutional reform) are needed for Bosnia and Herzegovina to move on compared to 25.10% who felt they are not. These findings answer another important question at the crux of this research. The statistics above show that respondents felt that the Strategy's proposed measures are legitimately needed and therefore can be instrumental in fostering reconciliation.

I would argue that these findings are a clear indication that the five key areas are on target with what members of the general populace (at least from this sample set) believe needs to happen for Bosnia and Herzegovina to address the past and move on. This resonates relates with what was discussed earlier about civil society and government being able to accurately address what is needed to help society move on. Chapter one explained that there were public consultations that were held with a variety of public, civic, and government actors to hammer out the framework for identifying the most important areas that needed to be addressed. In this aspect, the consultations were successful. The Strategy's proposed measures match the needs of the people it is supposed to help move on. 90% of those polled during UNDP-BiH's aforementioned research project on access to public perspectives indicated that they would support a strategy designed for facing issues from the past and seeking truth about the vents that occurred during the war (UNDP-BiH, 2011, p. 21).

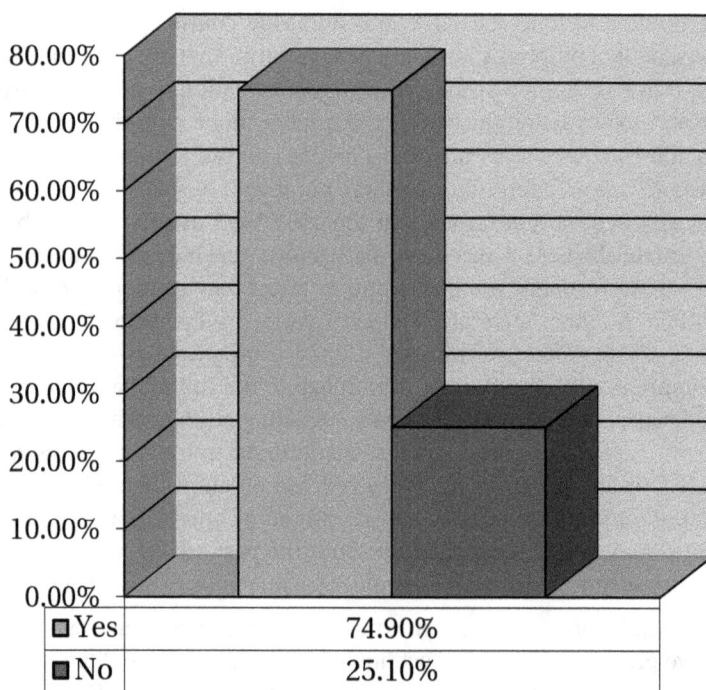

☐ Yes	74.90%
▣ No	25.10%

Figure 4. Summary of responses to survey question 4: Do you think the above processes are needed for Bosnia and Herzegovina to move forward from its past?

I believe these two sets of findings show that everyday Bosnians are eager from some type of comprehensive plan to address the past, that seemingly goes beyond the judicial mechanisms used. The state of non-transitional judicial mechanism as I noted in chapter six has been largely fragmented and uncoordinated by civil society actors. While civil society actors can play a major role in assisting the state in fulfilling its obligations; their roles are limited in an all actuality. Civil society organizations cannot deal with the official legal aspects of doling out reparations, for instance, or create laws that lead to institutional reform. These issues must be addressed by the State.

Furthermore, Fisher and Petrović-Ziemer (2013) conducted a series of interviews between March 2010 to April 2012 in countries impacted by the Yugoslav wars: Bosnia, Croatia, and Serbia. They found that interviewees from civil society actors in Bosnia and Herzegovina articulated more fervently than in other countries that people face the legacies of the recent past in private, social and political life to such a degree that it can hardly be ignored. The interviews also emphasized that intense media reporting on war crimes prosecutions, exhumations and funerals are a daily reality and a remember of the not so distant past. As someone who has lived in Sarajevo for almost two years, I can attest how rampant war crimes arrest and discourse are present in everyday reality for Bosnians. Moreover, the interviewees further note that in public, war victims and veterans claim their rights and involve themselves in commemoration events, many of which remain divisive. All these events and activities evoke memories of the violent past (Fisher and Petrović-Ziemer, 2013). It is examples like these that illustrate the need for other processes and mechanisms outside of judicial mechanisms to address these issues and the Strategy offers some of them. For instance, memorialization remains a very divisive issue in Bosnia and Herzegovina, because there is still a lack of agreed upon facts for the whole society to memorialize. The strategy was designed to include both elements. I believe that respondents may have viewed this Strategy's proposed mechanisms as a more encompassing approach to address Bosnia and Herzegovina's post-conflict issues.

Based on the data in Figure 5, it is clear that the majority of respondents believed that Institutional reform was the most important at 68.83%, followed by truth-telling at 64.44%, rehabilitations at 21.34%, then compensation at 12.55%, and finally remembrance at 14.23%. Also, these findings point to which key transitional justice mechanisms Bosnians prioritize the most. In the analysis of these particular findings, I want to pay particular attention to institutional reform, rehabilitation, and compensation. I have prioritized these due to the fact that I explored the importance of truth-telling and memory in the analysis for question four. Moreover, I believe these findings point to the importance of institutional reform the perspective of everyday Bosnians corresponds with and legitimizes much of the information that this research was based upon (as evidenced in chapters one and two), especially concerning Bosnia's current political climate.

For instance, as noted in earlier chapters, Bosnia and Herzegovina's governing institutions are regarded by many as being corrupt, inept, and dysfunctional, so I do not believe that the findings from this particular survey question should be a surprise. To support this claim, I present more relative data from UNDP-BiH's (2011) special report discussed earlier, when asked to what extent respondents agreed to all persons accountable for war crimes being banned from public office, 88.3% of those polled agreed, while 11.7% did not (UNDP-BiH, 2011, p. 22). These findings demonstrate that everyday citizens support institutional reforms like vetting. However, these sentiments do not necessarily match up to reality.

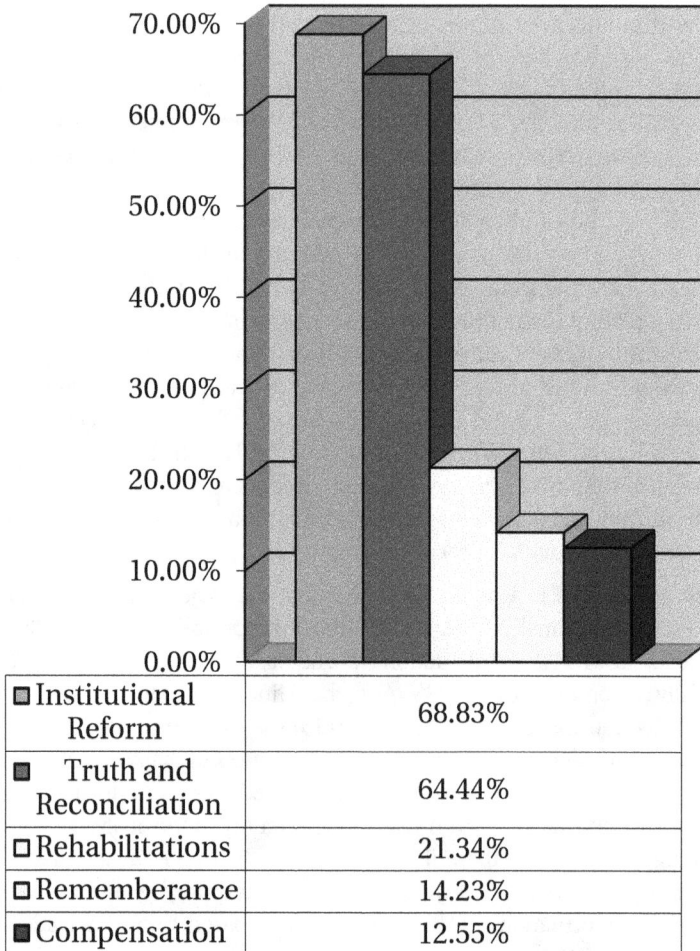

▣ Institutional Reform	68.83%
▣ Truth and Reconciliation	64.44%
▢ Rehabilitations	21.34%
▢ Rememberance	14.23%
▪ Compensation	12.55%

Figure 5. Summary of responses to survey question 5: Which of the five processes do you think is the most important out of the five key areas mention in question for reconciliation to take place in Bosnia and Herzegovina? Check more than one if it applies.

In October 2016, voters elected five people who were convicted of war crimes, corruption, kidnapping and abuse of office have been elected as mayors in municipal polls in Bosnia and Herzegovina (Kureljusić, 2016). The current Bosnian electoral law allows people who past war crimes convictions to seek office, except for those who have been charged by the former ICTY in the Hague (Kureljusić, 2016). People who are serving jail time doled out by any Bosnian court for war crimes cannot run for office, but after they are released, they are legally permitted (Kureljusić, 2016). I believe that ethno-politics play a role in these elections of formerly convicted war criminals. As I noted earlier, different ethnic groups see the outcome of the trials different, so while an individual may have been charged and served jail time that does not mean those who will elect him will consider the charges or the prison sentence legitimate. Again, war criminals have been known to receive a hero's welcome or veneration.

I would argue that there exists a difference with the prioritization of institutional reform over to the rest of the key areas because the other key areas are predicated on institutional reform. For instance, in order for the government to be able to deliver on compensation and rehabilitation, the institutions must be reformed in order to accomplish this tasks. Institutional reform will never happen also and as there remains a fractured political system that is subject to ethnic politics on every decision.

Compensation for war traumas and rehabilitation I believe are interconnected. Without proper compensation, many victims who live with war traumas may not be able to afford proper rehabilitation. Compensation can also be given in the form of rehabilitation services as well. Bosnia and Herzegovina currently lack a comprehensive plan to compensate victims or for rehabilitation, which was why they were included as part of the National Transitional Justice Strategy. A good example of the failures of lack of coordination for compensations is evidenced by the fact that hundreds of wartime survivors have received large fines after their reparation claims were rejected by courts in the Republika Srpska.

Furthermore, the issue stems from Bosnian authorities' failure to develop a nationwide law covering victims of torture, resulting in differing treatment of reparation claims in the Federation of Bosnia and Herzegovina and the Republika Srpska. Denying the right to reparation is in contradiction with the to the 2005 UN Basic Principles and Guidelines on the Right to a Remedy and Reparation for Victims of Gross Violations of International Human Rights Law and Serious Violations of International Humanitarian Law. Victims of gross human rights violations and serious violations of humanitarian law have the right to adequate, effective and prompt reparation for their harms. No national or entity level law should impede the victim's right to justice by the placement of statutes of limitations on reparations claims, nor should they be penalized.

 Part of institutional reform also means reforming the Dayton system as well. Transitional Justice measures will likely continue to be delayed or unrealized, as along as justice continues to be ethno-politicized. The current political system allows for this to happen. As I noted before that ethnic tensions do exists on issues related to the war and thereafter, but the current political system does not help ease those tensions either, when ethnicity is entrenched into it. Political wranglings between the two Entities' leaders as noted in chapter one, was one of the key reasons why the National Transitional Justice Strategy never materialized beyond the drafting of the document by an expert working group and a few debates in parliament.

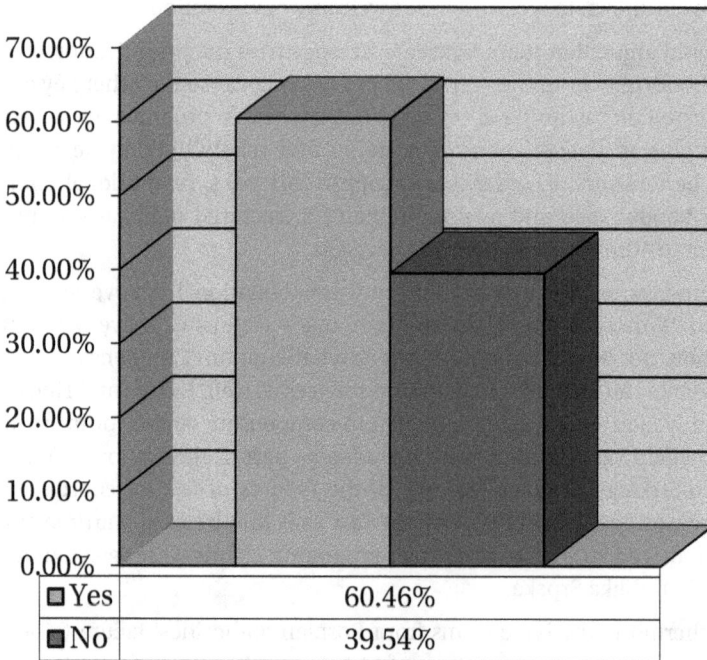

☐ Yes	60.46%
☐ No	39.54%

Figure 6. Summary of responses to survey question 6: Do you think reconciliation in Bosnia and Herzegovina is possible period?

The data in this graph shows that the majority of respondents at 60.46% felt that Bosnia and Herzegovina could move beyond its past compared to 39.54% who believed it could not. These statistics show that reconciliation is possible in the Bosnia and Herzegovina period. The data from this question is rather important because it shows that the majority of respondents believe the country can move forward. What good would it be to explore whether or not a strategy can foster reconciliation from the perspective of the people it is aimed at helping if those people do not think reconciliation is possible in general?

I also find the results from this to be very interesting, especially since there is often a misconception in conflict literature that many in Bosnia and Herzegovina do not want to reconcile ills of the past or that the country is sorely divided. In some cases, this is true. But, not everywhere in the country are there villages, towns, or cities filled with people seething with anger. So, newly produced data stands as a major contribution to the literature on reconciliation and Bosnia and Herzegovina that provides another perspective based on recently collected data. I would argue that it bears close ties to results discussed in the study done by Wilkes et al. (2012) that is also discussed in chapter 6, which found that 88.2% of respondents felt that a process of building trusting and honest relationships would be important for Bosnia and Herzegovina's future.

From the results of both studies, it becomes evident that there are those who are committed to the idea of reconciliation and that it is a necessary process for the country to move on. However, whether or not Bosnians believe reconciliation has occurred is another question. A 2013 study, commissioned by the United Nations Resident Coordinator's Office in Bosnia and Herzegovina, based on a total of 1,500 interviews conducted across the country found that the majority of the respondents do not think that the process of reconciliation in BiH has been completed (UNRCO-BiH, 2013, p. 25). The majority of the respondents also thought either that there was no reconciliation in BiH, or they described the extent of reconciliation as small or partial (UNRCO-BiH, 2013, p. 25). The study also notes that there are particular differences on views about reconciliation depending on the ethnicity of respondents. For instance, Serbs thought that there was little or no reconciliation in Bosnia and Herzegovina in comparison to Bosniaks and Croats. On the contrary, Bosniaks and Croats thought more often than Serbs that there is a certain progress in reconciliation in this country, whereby Croats are more convinced in this than Bosniaks (UNRCO-BiH, 2013, p. 25). I argue that we see these differing attitudes because many Serbs see the ICTY and domestic prosecutions were unfair and unreasonably targeted Serbs.

However, this is not something that is unique to the Bosnian context of reconciliation. In Rwanda, there were also differing opinions on justice and reconciliation based on ethnicity. Lambourne (2003) maintains that the majority of Hutu, the accused and their relatives, would have understandably also had very different attitudes towards justice and reconciliation compared to that of the Tutsi who largely saw themselves as victims (p. 25). Many Hutus were critical of the lack of justice for the alleged atrocities committed against Hutus by the Tutsi army, as well as of the arrest and detention without trial of many Hutu civilians (Lambourne, 2003). Many claimed that the legal justice and reconciliation needs of the Hutu majority were not being met by this process (Lambourne, 2003).

I moved to Sarajevo almost a year and a half after conducting this research, and I have to say that most people I have encountered in this city just want to move on and live their lives. Some research has indicated that perceptions in rural areas are often different from urban areas, arguing that reconciliation in some of these parts seems almost completely elusive. This could be due to the fact that many programs and initiatives for reconciliation are usually targeted towards urban populations more often. No matter the ethnicity, it is common to find people of all ethnic groups mixing and living life. What I believe has happened and is happening, is everyday reconciliation. Obradović and Howarth explain (2016) that the term everyday reconciliation focuses on the ways in which daily encounters with social and political representations of the past can be re-interpreted to create more nuanced images of conflicts and foster more critical and aware future generations. For many younger Bosnians their main concerns are not the blights of the past, but the growth of a new future that includes job opportunities and economic growth. That also includes a country which has a political system that no longer encourages division between its ethnic groups. As I noted in chapter four, reconciliation is a process. A large part of moving beyond the past has been indicated by the results from questions four and five is predicated on establishing an official truth.

The data in Figure 7 shows that the majority of respondents at 93.17% felt that the Government of Bosnia and Herzegovina could not lead the efforts compared to those who thought it could at 6.83%. The data from this question also correspond with the information discussed in the background and literature review about the Government of Bosnia and Herzegovina not being adequate. These sentiments are echoed in the survey results. The results from this question are important because the strategy created would be government-led, and if they had no faith in the government, how could they then have faith in the strategy? This also coincides with the data found from the results of question five, which found that the majority of respondents felt that institutional reform was the most important area of the strategy.

I believe these findings also mirror what was discussed throughout chapter six concerning the Government of Bosnia and Herzegovina's track record with creating and executing adequate transitional justice mechanisms. People seemingly have no faith in the government's ability to be able to do what it says it is going to do. To buttress these sentiments, I present more data the from the UNDP's special report, where they found that 60.3% of Bosnians do not trust their judiciary compared to 38.7% who do. This is extremely alarming given the fact that the judiciary should be the strongest, most independent, and well-respected institution in a democratic society.

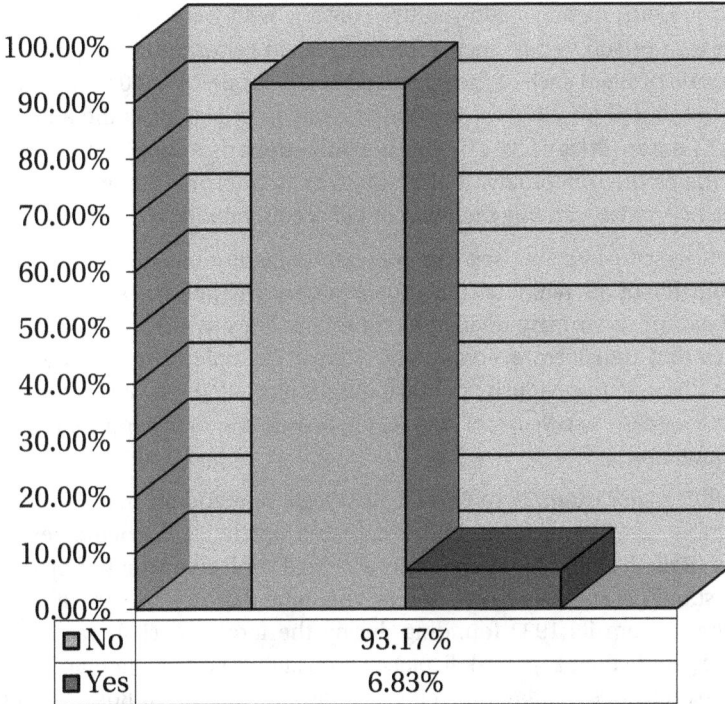

☐ No	93.17%
☐ Yes	6.83%

Figure 7. Summary of responses to survey question 7: If you believe reconciliation is possible, do you have faith in the Bosnian government to lead the efforts of reconciliation?

Considering the state of the judiciary and the struggle to prosecute war crimes adequately and in an efficient manner, it is not surprising that many Bosnians feel this. These sentiments are not confined to Bosnia and Herzegovina alone, according to Hrlović (2013) a survey conducted on respect for judicial institutions as early as 2001 found that in Croatia, 44.52% of citizens did not have confidence in courts, while 57% do not believe that there is rule of law in Croatia, and in Serbia, only 15% of citizens express confidence in the judiciary (p. 22). In societies where institutions are still developing, many citizens are unwilling to trust them, until proven otherwise. Especially when corruption and nepotism run rampant.

While judicial and legal institutions have become stronger in both Croatia and Serbia, in Bosnia and Herzegovina they have not. To illustrate why many Bosnians do not trust the legal institutions I present research by the Balkan Investigative Reporting Network, which established that cantonal courts and the Basic Court in Brčko allowed five convicts who were sentenced to up to one year in prison to pay fines in order to avoid prison time (Brkanić, 2016). The courts ordered each of the convicted to pay around 18,400 euros, a calculation estimated on the basis on that one day in prison costs the authorities about 51 euros (Brkanić, 2016). This not only supports impunity, but it always undermines the rule of law. It also shows to victims and the general society that war criminals can buy their way out of accountability.

When we consider the Bosnian context, its institutions are still struggling even outside of the realm of transitional justice. The political system as again noted earlier, is strongly divided along ethnic lines, which impacts creating policies that transform everyday life. A great example of this is the census results discussed previously; political infighting stalled the release of census results for nearly two years, of course, the census is simply supposed to count the population.

Another major example to posit is the illegal referendum that was held on September 25, 2016, the semi-by autonomous Serb led entity of the Republika Srpska (Bell, 2016). "The referendum was held to decide whether or not the entity should celebrate its own official "national day" on January 9th, a date that draws from its 1992 founding during the ferocious civil war that cost 100,000 people their lives and displaced thousands of others. January 9th is an orthodox religious holiday which the Constitutional Court of Bosnia and Herzegovina ruled was unconstitutional, citing that it was unfair to the other ethnicities" (Bell, 2016, para. 1).

While this referendum was illegal and condemned by the international community, there was no major recourse by State authorities. The Prosecutor's Office of Bosnia and Herzegovina's located in Sarajevo requested that the President of the Republika Srpska and the architect of the referendum, Milorad Dodik, come for questioning, but by the end of 2016 and as of early 2017 he seemingly continued to evade questioning and or any repercussions for breaking the law or violating the constitution. When all this is taken into consideration, it is therefore not surprising that people have very little faith in the government to do anything positive in moving the country forward from the past, when the government does not really function to meet create and or maintain strong institutions that ensure that the country runs fairly and justly.

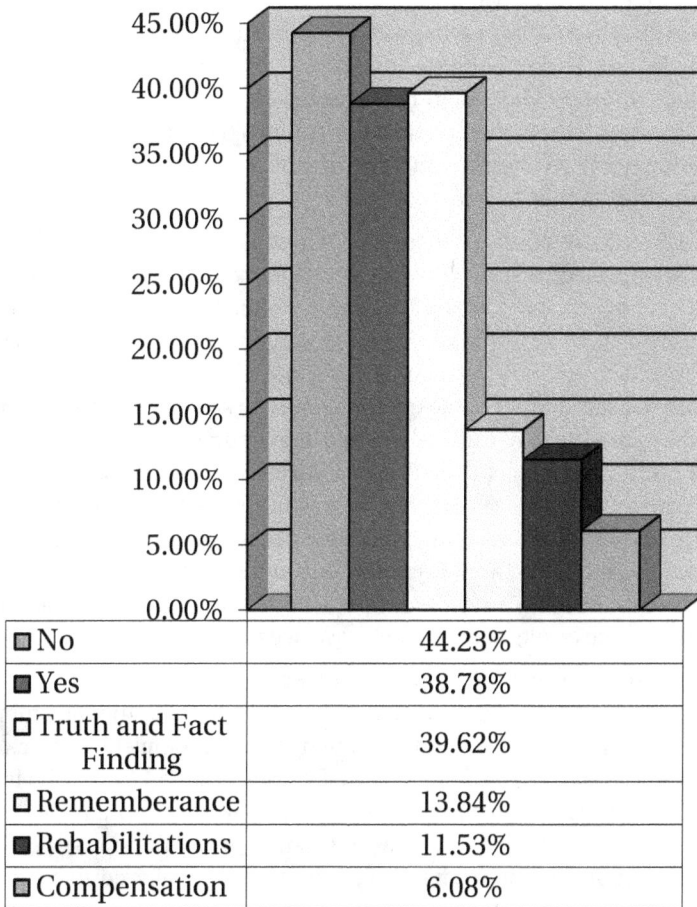

☐ No	44.23%
◼ Yes	38.78%
☐ Truth and Fact Finding	39.62%
☐ Rememberance	13.84%
◼ Rehabilitations	11.53%
☐ Compensation	6.08%

Figure 8. Summary of responses to question 8: Will activities in these key areas impact you or your family personally? If yes, which ones? Check more than one if more than one applies.

The data in this chart demonstrates that the majority of respondents at 42.23% of people would not be impacted by these key areas compared to those that said they would be at 38.78%. Those who said they would be impacted indicated they would be impacted the most by truth-telling at 39.62%, remembrance at 13.84%, then rehabilitations at 11.53%, and finally compensation at 6.08%. The results show that the majority of respondents will not be impacted; however, it is not a huge margin between those who are impacted and who are not impacted. From this information, one can imply that this

Strategy's mechanisms will not play a central part in the respondents' lives who said they would not be impacted versus those who said they would be impacted. Next, it is imperative to point out that truth-telling may be more important to those who would be impacted by the conflict directly. As has been discussed repeatedly throughout earlier chapters, the truth remains elusive for many in Bosnia and Herzegovina, and the responses from this question support this notion.

Also, I find these results particularly interesting, especially since those who would be impacted versus those who would not be impacted are quite statistically close. Perhaps those who will not be impacted by these five key areas may be impacted in other ways; as discussed earlier, post-conflict societies have many aspects to address, justice only being one of them. In reviewing the findings from the second part of the question, one can see that the majority of people will be impacted by truth-telling and remembrance. This reverts back to what was discussed earlier about the need to establish truth about the war and where remembrance hinges. It is also interesting to see that many were impacted more by truth and fact finding initiatives than they were by rehabilitation and compensation programs, especially due to the brutalities of the war. However, perhaps had there been a bigger population sample or another sample in a different city, the results may very well have been different.

Of the study participants (Figure 9), 44.81% felt that participating in the above activities (truth and fact finding, reparations, rehabilitation, and remembrance) or receiving compensation would help them move on completely, while 43.07% said it would help them move on eventually, compared to 12.12% who felt they would never be able to move on at all. This question is important, and the results speak to the overall question as to whether or not the strategy can foster reconciliation. According to the results, most people believed they would be able to move on then completely after participating in one of the above areas of the strategy. This rather implies that the majority of respondents have faith in the strategy's core areas to help them move on from the past.

I believe that these results show that there is a "ripeness" for reconciliation for many of the respondent and that if the past is properly dealt with, then there are those who can and will move on. Zartman (2003) further explains that "ripeness" happens as "parties resolve their conflict only when they are ready to do so—when alternative, usually unilateral, means of achieving a satisfactory result are blocked and the parties feel that they are in an uncomfortable and costly predicament" (para. 2). At that "ripe" moment, they seek or are amenable to proposals that offer a better way forward (Zartman, 2003). However, I do not want to indicate by my previous statements that the transitional justice mechanism laid out in this strategy can be a panacea for all of Bosnia and Herzegovina's post-conflict ills because as I mentioned in chapter one, this will not be the case. Yet these mechanisms seemingly do address some key issues that citizenry in Bosnia and Herzegovina need to move on, as is evidenced by responses to questions three and four. However, reconciliation is not a linear process; it happens at different paces and lengths when both individuals and communities are ready for it as I borrowed from Zartman's "ripeness" theory earlier.

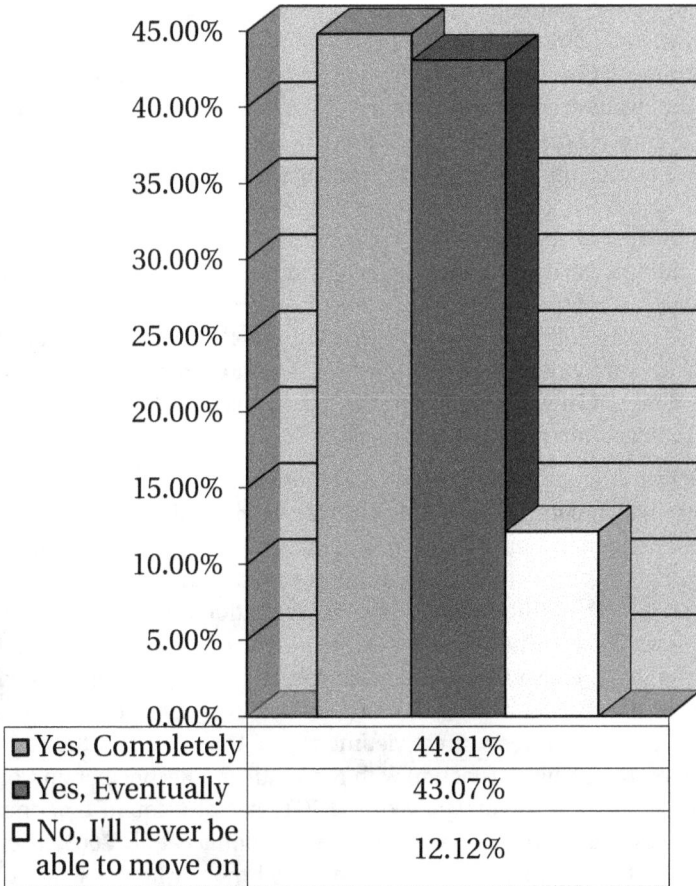

▣ Yes, Completely	44.81%
▣ Yes, Eventually	43.07%
▢ No, I'll never be able to move on	12.12%

Figure 9. Summary of responses to question 9: Will participating in any of the above activities or receiving any of benefits help you personally be able to reconcile the past and move on?

However, I argue that reconciliation and moving beyond the past are just as much of an individual process as it is a collective one, regardless of the transitional justice mechanisms used. As we have seen from the sentiments following the ICTY domestic trials in Bosnia and Herzegovina, transitional justice have left many victims feeling not vindicated. Interestingly enough, the UNDP-BiH's (2011) special report notes that when they asked respondents in their study how important were the events to them personally that took place during Bosnia and Herzegovina's 1992-1995 war that 36.4% of respondents answered that the events were very important and that they would never forget, while 35.4% of those polled responded that the events were important but that they have moved on with their lives (UNDP, 2011, p. 16). Many people are moving on with their lives, while many others have not. Reconciling the events of the past is a personal choice, not just a socio-political one. As I noted earlier in this chapter, I believe that everyday reconciliation is taking place in Bosnia and Herzegovina. But, I also believe that there must be proper measures developed and sanctioned by the State to help citizens also move on too. Aguilar et al. maintains within the Spanish context following the Francoist era that individuals have not seemingly just moved on or forgotten their history and the mere passage of time does not necessarily contribute to oblivion (p. 1412). They note that in Spain, the lack of appropriate transitional justice measures may have prevented victims and their relatives from leaving the past (Aguilar et al., 2011). I believe has been the case of moving beyond the past in Bosnia and Herzegovina as well.

Moreover, it is important to note that there are different factors that come into play which contribute to how individuals view what transitional justice methods are appropriate for reconciliation and which are not. The majority of respondents noted in their answers to question eight that neither them or their families would be impacted by the transitional justice measures proposed in this draft. Indivdual experiences and even experiences of family members and friends play an important role in shaping perspectives on transitional justice. In South Africa, Backer (as cited in Aguilar, 2003) found significant differences between direct victims of the Apartheid and the rest of the population regarding satisfaction with the Truth and Reconciliation Commission. In Rwanda, a survey study of the ICTJ has also found that "personal experiences shaped respondents' attitudes" (Thomas et al., 2008, as cited in Aguilar et al.). Perhaps, if I would have polled those who considered themselves direct or indirect victims responses about the proposed transitional justice measures helping them move on would be different.

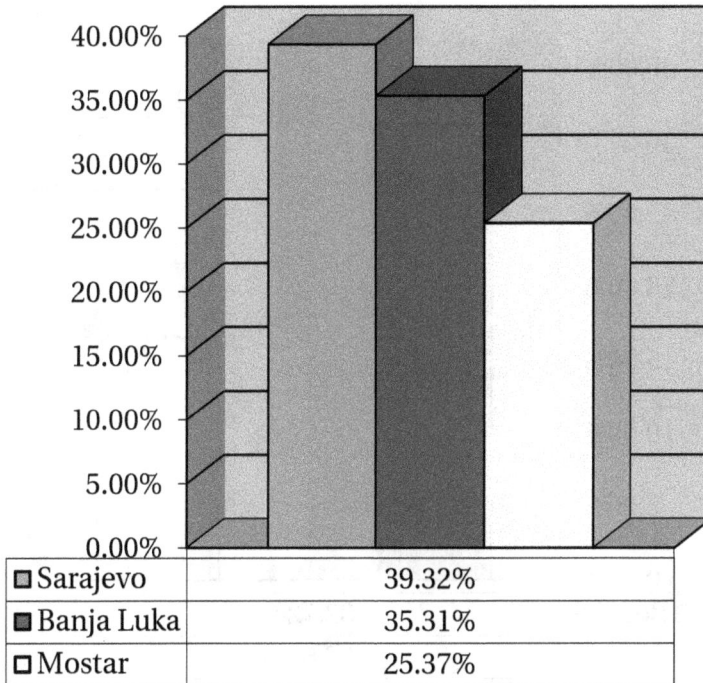

▣ Sarajevo	39.32%
▣ Banja Luka	35.31%
▢ Mostar	25.37%

Figure 10. Summary of responses to question 10: Which city do you live in?

The results of this question were very important because the study functioned on obtaining data from each city for comparison purposes. Based on the data in this chart, the majority of the respondents came from Sarajevo at 39.32%, while the second largest group of respondents came from Banja Luka at 35.31%, and finally, the fewer came from Mostar at 25.37%. The data implications are simple: the more populous cities had comparatively more participants. This sample is representative of the demographics discussed concerning each city size in chapter three. Having more participants allowed for a broader view of each city concerning ethnicity, gender, and age. This background information, of course, does have an impact on the results of all the survey questions. One cannot establish definitive trends because the numbers are not evenly distributed among cities. It is interesting to consider whether the demographics would have been different if the survey had been taken offline. Perhaps had I been in the field more people would have been willing and able to participate.

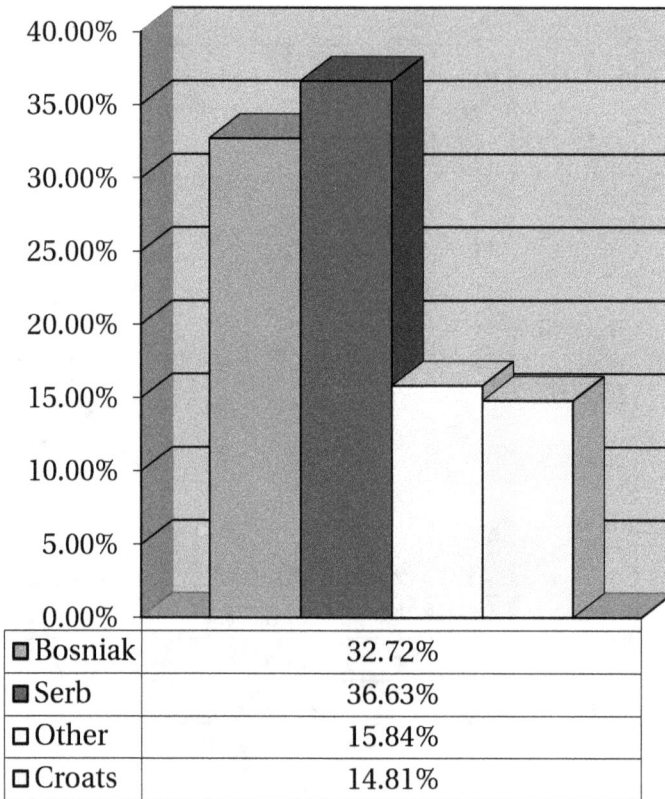

◘ Bosniak	32.72%
◼ Serb	36.63%
◻ Other	15.84%
◻ Croats	14.81%

Figure 11. Summary of responses to question 11: What ethnicity do you consider yourself?

The results of this question are extremely important because we can compare responses across ethnicity. Based on the data in this chart, the majority of respondents were Serb at 36.63%, while the second largest group of respondents were Bosniak at 32.72%, followed by those who considered themselves Other at 15.84%, and then finally those who considered themselves Croat at 14.81%. These results have important implications for the data, especially for those skeptics who often argue that Bosnia and Herzegovina cannot move on from ethnic conflict. These results show that respondents of all ethnicities were interested in the survey. Reverting back to question five that asked respondents if they believed Bosnia and Herzegovina could move, one realizes that the majority said yes, they believed it could. This finding reveals that the majority of respondents across ethnic lines agree that Bosnia and Herzegovina can reconcile. This logic can also be applied to the results of question three as well, where it asks respondents if they believed that the five areas address what is needed for the country to move on.

I especially found these findings to be extremely interesting, given that there are often so many differing opinions among the different ethnicities on transitional justice in Bosnia and Herzegovina. However, Serbs may be the majority of those who participated in the survey because of how the keywords were marketed. There were more keywords to market the survey that would have caught Serbs attention versus that of the Bosniak or Croats and those listed as other. Especially considering the fact that the majority of respondents were Serbs, there is a common conception that Serbs are not as interested in issues related to addressing war crimes in Bosnia because Serbs often seem to be demonized for being the aggressors of the conflict.

Furthermore, I would have surely thought Bosniaks would have been the majority since Sarajevo is the most populous city and is largely comprised of Bosniaks. I am also surprised that there were many people who identified as Other. This may be because in Bosnia in Herzegovina, many people who are of mixed marriages do not consider themselves any one ethnicity and so they fall outside the mainstream classifications; this is also the case for Jews and Roma people. In any case, I believe these results show that people of all ethnicities believe they have a stake in transitional justice, regardless of the attacks on the processes by political elites. One of the key questions, is then why this interest has not materialized into more direct pressure and action on the political elites and government institutions to implement this strategy and other forms of transitional justice? I believe it goes back to what I mentioned before about people being wary about trusting the government to actually be effective in implementing transitional justice.

I would argue another major part of the answer to this question is that many people in Sarajevo and beyond from what I have found are just trying to survive day by day, in a country with high unemployment and limited economic growth, perhaps they feel if their energy is to be used collectively then it should be used to address these things, rather than trying to get their government to address the past. Another part of the answer goes back to political will and political culture.

Everyday Bosnians have not yet developed a strong sense of political activism as I discussed earlier, many social and political ills are met with apathy. Many times, when I have raised issues about inconsistencies in policies and laws concerning almost just about anything, I'm met with the same answer of "well this is Bosnia, what do you expect". It is as people accept the dysfunctions of their political and economic systems. Sadly, pushing for adequate and effective post-conflict justice is approached the same way. Responding to a survey is a completely different world from making one's sentiments expressed on that survey a reality, especially if one does not feel empowered.

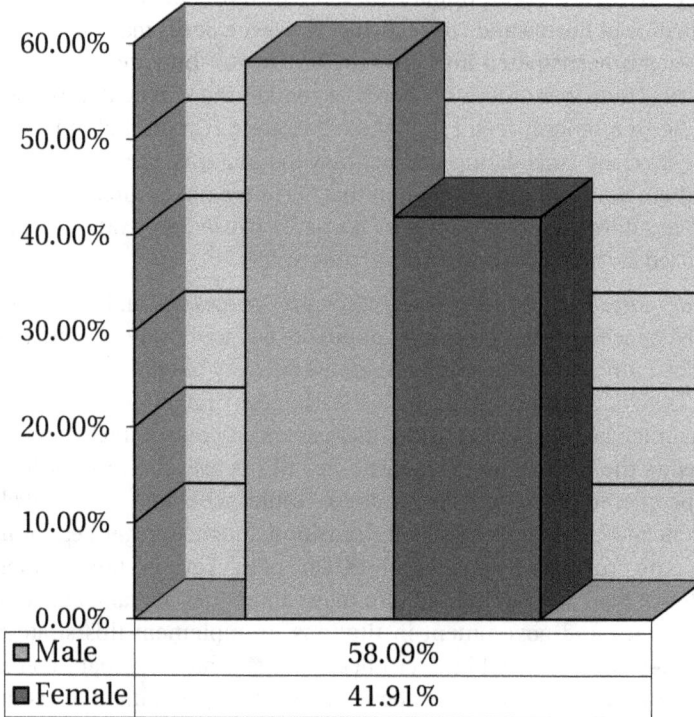

Figure 12. Summary of response to question 12: What is your gender?

Based on the data in this chart, the majority of respondents were male at 58.09% compared to those who were female at 41.91%. The fact that more men responded corresponds with the fact that there are more men across the age range in which the survey is set. The results of this question are important because they allow the researcher to be able to compare other data in relation to gender and how the participants view different aspects of the Transitional Justice Strategy.

Also, another factor to consider is that a lot of transitional justice mechanisms that have been attempted have left women's issues largely out of the process, so perhaps some women were less likely to be motivated to participate in this study. As discussed in the in chapter five, many women were victims of rape or other forms of violence, and there has been little done to address those atrocities. Many sexual violence crimes are slow to be prosecuted, and many women still live without the socio-psychological support they need. As noted in chapter one, there are other strategies that have been developed to deal with women's issues in post-war Bosnia and Herzegovina. However, as was discussed earlier, many of these strategies have yet to be executed successfully. Many victims of rape are ashamed to come forward due to stigma and also a lack of resources to help them deal with the past.

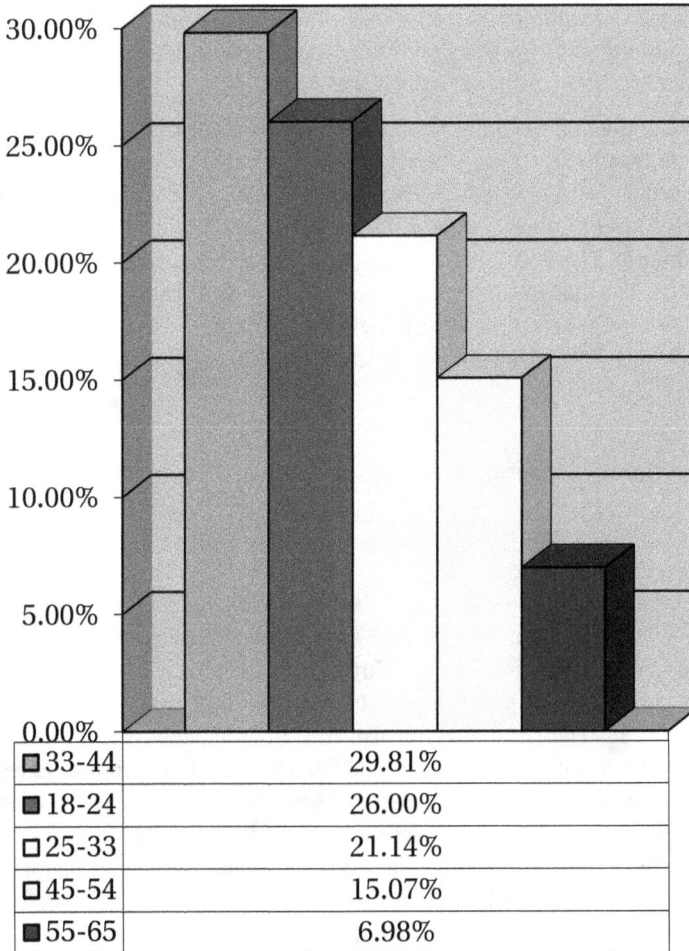

■ 33-44	29.81%
■ 18-24	26.00%
□ 25-33	21.14%
□ 45-54	15.07%
■ 55-65	6.98%

Figure 13. Summary of responses to question 13: What is your age range?

This question was designed to inquire about the age of the participants. Based on these data in this chart, one sees that the majority of respondents were between the ages of 33-44 at 29.81%, the second largest group of respondents was between the ages of 18-24 at 26%, then the third largest group of respondents was ages 25-33 at 21.14%, the fourth largest group of respondents was ages 45-54 at 15.07%, and the smallest group of respondents was ages 55-65 at 6.98%.

I would argue that the majority of respondents were between the ages of 33 and 44 because I believe their lives were perhaps the most impacted by the war; they can remember life both before and after the war. Age plays an important role and has an impact on the results , many people who lived through the war versus those who did not may have very different responses. So, it is important to remember that during the early 1990s, many people in the age bracket 33-44 were middle school age, late teens to early 20s.

I would argue that they had more interest in this idea of the Transitional Justice Strategy and the survey because the war they saw impacted most of their youth, teenage, and early adult years, unlike some of the younger respondents who were either just born or some of the older respondents who remember life before the war. There was a drop in respondents as the ages get older and older due to the fact that this was an internet survey. As I discussed before, many older Bosnians may not use computers and therefore do not have access to Facebook and other social media outlets where the survey was marketed.

Hypotheses Test Results

In this section appear results from the four hypotheses that were tested:

Test 1

With the p-value > below .05 at a Chi-Square value of 2.697, the null hypothesis is rejected. There is statistical significance; those participants who believed in the Transitional Justice Strategy are likely to believe that the Bosnian government's efforts will lead to reconciliation. These test determined that there is statistical significance; those participants who believe in the Transitional Justice Strategy are likely to believe that its proposed measures will foster reconciliation. If one believes that the strategy encompasses enough elements to help the country move forward, then why would one not believe the efforts would lead to reconciliation? The correlation makes perfect sense. As noted earlier, many of the core issues that the strategy addresses have been lacking at the State level since the end of war.

Table 1. Test 1 Crosstabulation

If you believe moving on is possible, do you have faith in the Bosnian government to lead the efforts to move on?					
			Yes	No	Total
The strategy focuses on five key areas for addressing the conflict in the 1990s, truth and fact finding, reparations, rehabilitation, memorialization, and institutional reform. Do you think these areas address the main issues that have stopped Bosnia and Herzegovina from moving on?		1	0	9	10
	Yes	24	19	200	243
	No	23	11	200	234
	Total	48	30	409	487

Table 2. Test 1 Chi-Square Analysis

	Value	df	Asymp. Sig. (2-sided)
Pearson Chi-Square	2.697[a]	4	.610
Likelihood Ratio	3.299	4	.509
N of Valid Cases	487		
Note. [a] *Two cells (22.2%) have expected count less than five. The minimum expected count is .62.*			

Test 2

With the p-value > above .05 at a Chi value of 6.610, the null is accepted. There is no statistically significant difference in the belief that it is possible for Bosnia and Herzegovina to move on between Bosniaks and Croats, and Serbs. I found this to be surprising, especially in the light of some of the current events that were discussed above. I initially thought there would be a major difference between respondents of different ethnic groups, especially since ethnic lines are so greatly visible in Bosnia and Herzegovina on issues relating to the war. I argue that this is a positive for moving on and again indicates the ripeness for reconciliation that I discussed earlier. However, interestingly enough, this question and nor does this research particularly ask what moving on actually means for participants. As noted earlier, there are conflicting views as to whether or not there has been reconciliation in Bosnia and Herzegovina. I argue that a major part of this is due to the fact a common and shared conception of what it means to move has not been officially developed across all ethnic groups.

Table 3. Test 2 Crosstabulation

Do you think moving beyond the past is possible period in Bosnia and Herzegovina?			Yes	No	Total
Combined - 2 (FILTER)	-1	0	93	85	178
	Selected	2	145	84	231
	Total	2	238	169	409

Table 4. Test 2 Chi-Square Analysis

	Value	df	Asymp. Sig. (2-sided)
Pearson Chi-Square	6.610[a]	2	.037
Likelihood Ratio	7.345	2	.025
N of Valid Cases	409		

Note. [a] Two cells (33.3%) have expected count less than five. The minimum expected count is .87.

Test 3

With a p-value > below .05 at a Chi-Square Value of 2.194, the null hypothesis is rejected. There is a significant statistical difference between those who believed that the government of Bosnia and Herzegovina can lead efforts towards reconciliation between respondents between the ages of 18 and 33 and respondents between the ages of 55 and 65. This makes sense due to the size of the sample of those respondents between the ages of 18 and 33 versus those between the ages of 55 and 65. Since an online survey was used as the primary tool for collecting data, as noted above, the elderly, more than likely do not have the skills to use a computer and therefore do not have access to social media where the survey was marketed. I also believe that younger Bosnians have a more negative view of their government compared to those who are older and lived through a different time period. The current system is all they currently political system is all they have experienced.

Table 5. Test 3 Crosstabulation

If you believe moving on is possible, do you have faith in the Bosnian government to lead the efforts to move on?					
			Yes	No	Total
Age range	2.00	25	10	188	223
	6.00	1	2	30	33
	Total	26	12	218	256

Table 6. Test 3 Chi-Square Analysis

	Value	df	Asymp. Sig. (2-sided)
Pearson Chi-Square	2.149^a	2	.334
Likelihood Ratio	2.806	2	.246
N of Valid Cases	256		
Note. [a] Two cells (33.3%) have expected count less than five. The minimum expected count is 1.55.			

Test 4

With the p-value > above .05 and a Chi-Square value of .675, the null hypothesis is accepted. There is no statistically significant difference in the belief that the drafts Transitional Justice Strategy's five key areas will be adequate in helping Bosnia and Herzegovina address its issues between men and women. I find this surprising also, considering the aforementioned topics of women, rape, war, and accountability. I anticipated that women may have wanted more in the Strategy concerning women's issues directly. As noted above and in chapter one, women were some of the easiest targets during the war. Also, many women lost sons, husbands, nephews, and brothers; so perhaps one of the key areas, like truth-telling or remembrance, carried a lot of weight.

Table 7. Test 4 Crosstabulation

What is your gender?		Female	Male	3	Total
The strategy focuses on five key areas for addressing the conflict in the 1990s, truth and fact finding, reparations, rehabilitation, memorialization, and institutional reform. Do you think these areas address the main issues blocking reconciliation?		4	6	0	10
	Yes	104	136	3	243
	No	94	138	2	234
	Total	202	280	5	487

Table 8. Test 4 Chi-Square Analysis

	Value	df	Asymp. Sig. (2-sided)
Pearson Chi-Square	.675[a]	4	.954
Likelihood Ratio	.775	2	.942
N of Valid Cases	487		
Note. [a] Four cells (44.4%) have expected count less than five. The minimum expected count is .10.			

Conclusion

The findings and the discussion in this chapter confirm some of the discourse and assumptions that were laid out in earlier chapters, but it also offers a nuanced discussion as well. I believe these results confirm that the current processes that have taken place surrounding post-conflict justice in Bosnia and Herzegovina have not been enough. Also, these findings confirm that many Bosnians are still eager to learn the truth about what happened in the Bosnian war between 1992 and 1995. I believe this research also shows that Bosnians do not have faith in their current institutions to lead the process of post-conflict justice or reconciliation. The exciting part of these findings is that it shows that Bosnians of all ethnic groups are interested in a process in which they can own themselves. The data also shows that the concept of Bosnia and Herzegovina moving beyond its past is not an impossible feat and that the country may not be as bitterly divided as often reported.

Chapter 10

Summary, Conclusions, and Lessons

Jared O. Bell

This chapter synthesizes, summarizes and concludes many of the main points that have been discussed throughout this book. Along with the summaries and conclusions, this chapter also reflects on key lessons we can draw from the failures of the Bosnian government that impeded upon implementation of the National Transitional Justice Strategy and their implications. I believe that these lessons are still applicable to Bosnia and Herzegovina currently, as well as other transitional justice contexts. This chapter will first summarize and synthesize three key overall themes on which this book has been focused: the process of post-conflict justice in Bosnia and Herzegovina to date, finally the process behind the creation of the National Transitional Justice Strategy, and then finally the state of reconciliation currently.

Post-Conflict Justice in Bosnia and Herzegovina

Overall, this book explores the process of post-conflict justice in general and whether or not the processes have led to reconciliation in Bosnia and Herzegovina. Post-conflict justice in Bosnia and Herzegovina has been an arduous journey, to say the least. The processes that have largely been used to confront crimes of the 1992-1995 war have been retributive in nature. Restorative measures have been attempted by civil society organizations, through community-based projects on truth-telling, but as a whole have not been very successful. The ICTY and the War Crimes Chamber in Bosnia and Herzegovina have been the two foremost ways that the crimes of the past have been addressed. The creation of the ICTY in 1993, was the first international tribunal since Nuremberg where the international community decided to address gross human rights violations such as war crimes, crimes against humanity, and genocide. The Tribunal sought to bring victims across the Former Yugoslavia a sense of justice and closure that they probably would not have had otherwise. After hundreds of testimonies and over a dozen convictions. The legacy of ICTY remains mixed. There are those who hail the ICTY as a major global institution that set a groundbreaking precedent against impunity and enforced accountability. It is undeniable that the process of the ICTY has led to the largest collection of information about a conflict in history. This by itself to me is a huge feat and a major precedent in history. Generations after this one will be able to know what happened in the Former Yugoslavia and the Bosnian war in the early to mid-90s. The crimes committed will forever be a part of record history.

However, on the other hand, there are those who believe that the ICTY was a series of show trials who sought out to punish some groups' war crimes over that of others. There are those who still maintain that the ICTY was an imposed form of justice from the international community. The ICTY did not foster reconciliation in Bosnia and Herzegovina, but it is often argued that it was not the main purpose for the Tribunal. It is also often argued that the ICTY's lengthy trials, conducted so far from the scene of the crimes and the victims impacted by them had a limited reach from the beginning. One fact I believe that remains clear is that the proceedings of the ICTY unfortunately did not unite people in Bosnia and Herzegovina, but they divided them instead. Despite the official record, there has been no official agreement on the full facts of the crimes committed in the territory of Bosnia and Herzegovina. However, no matter if we take the good with the negatives of the ICTY, I believe we will see the full impact of its legacy in time. While that might be cliché, I believe future generations will make their own conclusions about the ICTY and its work in Bosnia and Herzegovina and elsewhere in the Former Yugoslavia.

The War Crimes Chamber in Bosnia and Herzegovina was developed in the mid-2000s , along with a National War Crimes Strategy designed to process the most important cases within 15 years. However, the National War Crimes Strategy has been slow in prosecuting war crimes, as the courts continue to lack proper coordination on both the State, entity, and local levels. War crimes prosecutions in Bosnia and Herzegovina like those prosecuted at the ICTY have been subject to attacks, as nationalistic politicians use proceedings as political fodder and continuously attack the courts and their rulings. Respect and trust for the courts of Bosnia and Herzegovina remain in peril. Many Bosnians remain disconnected from the process daily and hear about cases as they become politicized through political leaders and the media. The court today is not seen as a beacon for reconciliation or healing. Moreover, since the National War Crimes Strategy did not process the most important cases within the time limit set forward, there remains talk about revising the strategy to address the some of the most important cases within a new realistic time frame.

The National Transitional Justice Strategy

The key premise of this book was to explore how everyday Bosnians perceived The National Draft Transitional Justice Strategy's contents and whether or not they believed the proposed measures would foster reconciliation in Bosnia and Herzegovina. The National Transitional Justice Strategy was birthed to address the issues of the past that the retributive processes that took place at the ICTY and in the Courts of Bosnia and Herzegovina did not address. The five key areas this Strategy aimed to address in particular was truth and fact finding, institutional reform, rehabilitation, and compensation. The National Transitional Justice Strategy was developed by an expert working group that aimed to engage members of Bosnian civil society across the country and various groups representing different issues. The Strategy, unfortunately, became subjected to apathy, political infighting, and ethno-political musings of Bosnia and Herzegovina's leaders and the Strategy never went further than a draft with a few debates on taking place amongst the Council of Ministers. Any discussion of the strategy and its proposed measures have disappeared from the public sphere, with many everyday Bosnians never having heard of it or its proposed measures to help move the country forward.

The State of Reconciliation

One key mission of the research in this book was to gauge the perspective of Bosnians on the National Transitional Justice Strategy and its ability to foster reconciliation. Additionally, I also wanted to know if for everyday Bosnians moving beyond the past was an actual possibility, especially since reading in news and academic publications that there has been little to no reconciliation in Bosnia and Herzegovina. However, the state of reconciliation in Bosnia and Herzegovina remains complicated. As I noted earlier, throughout this book, that the definition of what reconciliation means in Bosnia and Herzegovina is still being defined. Reconciliation is caught in a web of competing truths about the 1992-1995 war, who is to blame, and how fair the justice process has been or has not been.

As I have demonstrated throughout this book, there remains an interest in transitional justice measures fostered by the State that encourages truth-telling, beyond the current facts that were uncovered during the war. While the facts have been gathered about the war, the facts have not been translated into a general Bosnian narrative. I believe that there is an attitude of positivity amongst everyday Bosnians, about moving beyond the past. As I noted earlier, the entirety of Bosnia and Herzegovina's political system discourages reconciliation, as its structures remain geared towards ethnic quotas and ethno-politics. However, beyond the pale of the political system, there are everyday Bosnians who are living their lives working together and who are now living as neighbors and friends regardless of ethnicity or the verdicts in the Courts of Bosnia and Herzegovina.

Conclusions and Lessons from This Research Study

This portion of the chapter will conclude four key points and lessons that we can draw from the research that was conducted. In the following section, six conclusions and their implications are discussed:

The first conclusion

It can be concluded that hypothetically from the view of respondents, the Transitional Justice Strategy's programs can foster reconciliation. The fact that the majority thought these processes were what is accurate and needed to move the country forward, and the majority also said that participating in activities related to the five key areas would help them move on almost immediately implies that the strategy is on track with what the majority of respondents believe is necessary for Bosnia and Herzegovina to address its past. However, it can also be concluded that from the view of respondents, truth-telling, fact finding, and institutional reform remain very important parts of the strategy for Bosnia and Herzegovina to move on. This deduction implies that these two issues must be addressed adequately before Bosnia and Herzegovina can definitively move on from its past.

However, there remains almost no discussion on this Strategy or any attempts at outreach currently. When I tried to find further research on the strategy after 2014-2015, I could not find anything substantial. As noted in chapter one, there was very little outreach beyond the five consultations and a few public events beyond 2012. No even relevant news has emerged either. The lack of public engagement remains one of the key reasons why this strategy was never implemented. Without public support drawn, there was no political will for political elites at the State or entity level to see the process through to implementation. Perhaps, eventually, some of these mechanisms will be implemented on their own individually. But, currently allocating the necessary human and financial resources to meet the targets of the current National War Crimes Strategy alone remains a challenge.

Lesson. What we can draw from this process is that proper outreach and public engagement is extremely important in not only designing but also implementing transitional justice processes. Public engagement not only helps the general public remain informed, but it allows them to take ownership of the process and come to the table as equal stakeholders. As I noted in chapter nine, with the example of the ICC's work in the Central African Republic that effective outreach can have a major impact on the way local populations come to understand and respect transitional justice processes.

Moreover, I also believe the case of Bosnia and Herzegovina shows us that while the international community can aid in the process of post-conflict justice and enforcing international human rights norms, it cannot take over the process entirely, it must be owned by the local population. Reconciliation, I argue, absolutely must be a process that is owned by local individuals. What I argued about the limitations of transitional in chapter three is applicable to fostering reconciliation in a post-conflict situation, while the international community can provide the expertise and financial resources that help societies design reconciliation programs or initiatives, but it cannot take part in fostering the healing. This must be done by citizens who want to move beyond the dark shadows of the past. While there are such citizens, they have to be engaged properly and invited to the table. As I proposed in chapter nine, there remains a plethora of ways to engage citizens that go beyond traditional in person consultations and round tables. Internet access, computers, smart phones, and other technologies are widely available. The State would be remiss not to take advantage of these opportunities as a means of outreach, that will engage everyday citizens and control the narrative from ethno-political/nationalistic leanings of politicians.

The second conclusion

It can be concluded that there is very little or no faith in the Bosnian government to lead the country's reconciliation efforts. This was something that all respondents and pretty much agreed upon regardless of the age, ethnicity, or city. As noted earlier, several times the track record for Bosnia and Herzegovina's Government and implementing transitional justice processes has been extremely poor or slow. The Government of Bosnia and Herzegovina's public image often discourages citizens from trusting or believing in its ability to address their current needs let alone the crimes of the past. I believe that it is this image that demotivates everyday Bosnians to be both socially and politically active on the whole. I also argue that this is another key reason the strategy failed. Many citizens (those that may have had knowledge of it) were probably unlikely to vest their time, energy and hope in trying to pressure their political elites into trying to implement another set of transitional justice measures that would not come to fruition in the end anyway.

The government of Bosnia and Herzegovina must do more to repair the image of State institutions in the general public's eyes. Beyond transforming the image of the Bosnian government, repairing the image of the State goes beyond just outreach on transitional justice measures. Rebuilding the public image of the State means that the State and those who lead it work for the benefit of all citizens and care about justice being served and maintained even if their particular ethnicity happens to be on the receiving end of it.

Lesson. One key lesson we can draw from this conclusion is that the perceived effectiveness of state institutions impacts whether or not people will invest their time and energy in looking the government to lead them on issues such as transitional justice, institutional reform, memorialization, etc. Without addressing major key issues through transforming key public, legal, and governance institutions, it is very unlikely that the perception of the government amongst everyday Bosnian citizens will change.

The third conclusion

It can be concluded that Bosnia and Herzegovina is capable of moving beyond its past, according to the perspective of many respondents. This conclusion is evidenced by looking at the research discussed in chapter six concerning the attitudes of Bosnians towards reconciliation along with the data collected from my survey and some of the other studies that I presented. This idea implies that ethnic divisions may not be as deeply entrenched among the vast majority of the population as is often discussed. However, the challenge is that there has been no definitive answer as to what moving on looks like. However, as the participants indicated in the survey results, the five key areas of the strategy (truth and fact finding, reparations, rehabilitation, memorialization, and institutional reform) are indeed needed to move on.

Lesson. No one transitional justice measure can or will foster reconciliation in a post-conflict society. Multiple mechanisms and measures should be utilized as they may address different needs of the different levels of society. While the retributive measures have been a key tool for accountability, restorative justice, and reparative justice measures can be used help people move on the consequences of the war that impact their daily lives. These tools are also needed to help foster deeper conversations about what reconciliation means and to what stage of reconciliation Bosnian society wants to reach. Retributive justice alone has not been able to do this.

Fourth and final conclusion

It can be concluded that with the lack of resources, as well as public and political support, this strategy will ever actually come to fruition. As noted earlier, transitional justice policies are public policies just like any other piece of legislation a government may introduce to spurn change.

Lesson. For any piece of policy to move forward, there must be the proper support and resources for it to do. This arguably the major reason why the Transitional Justice Strategy failed to materialize. As I noted earlier in this chapter's summary, political elites at both the State and entity level decided to stop attending meetings of the expert working group. While civil society has tried to gauge the public interests, their reach has been limited and not as impactful. Civil society is only one side of the coin, they can bring the voices of citizens to the State, but they cannot craft and implement policies that are reflective of the citizens they represent only the State can do this. The State's leaders must have the commitment and the interest to do this for the betterment of their nation and their constituencies lives.

Questions to Consider for Further Research

One key important question emerging from this research, which can be applied for any transitional justice context, is: if no one puts pressure on their politicians to implement these policies, then what are the consequences of not implementing them? Are there any? If more people know about and or believed that strategy could be implemented, perhaps they would put more pressure on their political elites and governing institutions to make the strategy a major public policy issue. But then again, the majority of respondents do not even have faith in their government to lead the efforts to begin with, as was discussed earlier, so what then would be the point in applying further political pressure to an institution that one feels is inadequate? As I noted earlier in this chapter, Bosnian authorities must rebuild the image of state institutions. But, how? These questions lay the foundation for further research on this particular topic.

Perhaps some elements of this study can be expanded for further research, also by looking at how location and ethnicity impact views on moving forward. For instance, do Bosniaks in Sarajevo feel the same as Bosniaks in Mostar or Banja Luka? Since the war, a lot of facts and truths have been uncovered about the conflict; so, for those who think that truth-telling and fact finding are important for Bosnia and Herzegovina moving on, what would that mean? And would they change their views of past events? Also, it would be interesting to find out if (and why) respondents would have had more faith in this strategy if it had been led by an international organization or agency.

While some of the topics discussed and questions raised in this book may not be able to be answered with ease or without much debate, they are important and worth asking by those in the field who want to aid those in societies that are trying to recover from the disasters of conflict. As we know, conflicts leave more than just physical wounds, they leave mental and emotional scars that last lifetimes. So, in exploring all options and ideas when trying to aid societies in post-conflict transition periods, professionals in this discipline are enabling them to address their wounds and scars of the past so they can write a better and much greater future of their nation and generations to come.

Bibliography

Ackerman, P., & DuVall, J. (2000). *A force more powerful: A century of nonviolent conflict.* New York: St. Martin's Press.

Aguilar, P., Balcells, L., & Cebolla-Boado, H. (2011). *Determinants of Attitudes Toward Transitional Justice.* Comparative Political Studies, 44(10), 1397-1430. doi:10.1177/0010414011407468

Ahmetašević, N. (2015, November 4). Bosnia's unending war. *The New Yorker.* Retrieved from http://www.newyorker.com/news/news-desk/bosnias-unending-war

Amnesty International. (2017). CROATIA 2016/2017. Retrieved December 26, 2017, from https://www.amnesty.org/en/countries/europe-and-central-asia/croatia/report-croatia/

Anderson, J. D. (2006). *Qualitative and quantitative research.* Retrieved from http://web20kmg.pbworks.com/w/file/fetch/82037432/QualitativeandQuantitativeEvaluationResearch.pdf

Balkans Investigative Network. (2017, February 6). First Serbian Srebrenica Trial Opens in Belgrade. Retrieved February 07, 2017, from http://www.balkaninsight.com/en/article/first-serbian-srebrenica-trial-opens-in-belgrade-02-06-2017

Banović, D. (2016). *Political culture in post-conflict and divided societies: The case of Bosnia and Herzegovina.* Available from Academia website: https://www.academia.edu/10234522/Political_Culture_in_PostConflict_and_Divided_Societies

Barsalou, J. (2005, April). Trauma and Transitional Justice in Divided Societies (Publication No. 135). Retrieved https://www.usip.org/sites/default/files/sr135.pdf

Bell, J. O. (2016, October 28). BiH Recent Political Strife Challenges the Narrative of the International Community's Ability to create long term Peace Building and Stability. Retrieved January 30, 2017, from http://www.sarajevotimes.com/?p=109462

Bieber, F. (2014). Serbs in Bosnia. In *Encyclopedia Princetoniensis: Princeton encyclopedia of self-determination.* Retrieved from https://pesd.princeton.edu/?q=node/242

Bosnia and Herzegovina Ministry for Human Rights and Refugees, Ministry of Justice, & Bosnia and Herzegovina Ministry of Justice. (2013). TRANSITIONAL JUSTICE STRATEGY FOR BOSNIA AND HERZEGOVINA 2012- 2016 (Bosnia and Herzegovina). Sarajevo.

Biruski, D. C. (2012). Lessons learned from the former Yugoslavia: The case of Croatia. In D. Landis & R. D. Albert (Eds.), *Handbook of ethnic conflict: International perspectives.* New York: Springer.

Brahm, E. (2009). What is a Truth Commission and Why Does it Matter? Peace & Conflict Review, 3, 2nd ser.

Brahm, E. (2013). *Transitional justice: A user guide to the beyond intractability system.* Retrieved from http://www.beyondintractability.org/userguide/transitional-justice

Brkanić, Dž. (2016, August 10). Bosnian War Crimes Convicts Pay to Stay Free. Retrieved April 27, 2018, from http://www.balkaninsight.com/en/article/bosnian-war-crimes-convicts-pay-to-stay-free-08-09-2016

Bytyci, F. (2017, February 13). Kosovo to form truth commission as wounds from 1998-99 war fester. Retrieved December 26, 2017, from https://www.reuters.com/article/uk-kosovo-president-commission/kosovo-to-form-truth-commission-as-wounds-from-1998-99-war-fester-idUKKBN15S1U5

Casmir, A., Diechtiareff, B., Letica, B., & Switzer, C. (2005). *An analysis of the Dayton negotiations and peace accords* [Final research paper]. Retrieved from http://ocw.tufts.edu/data/12/244825.pdf

Chapman, A. R. (2009). Approaches to studying reconciliation. In H. Van Der Merwe, V. Baxter, & A. R. Chapman (Eds.), *Assessing the impact of transitional justice: Challenges for empirical research* (pp. 143-172). Washington, DC: United States Institute of Peace.

Clark, P. (2010). *The Gacaca courts, post- genocide justice and reconciliation in Rwanda: Justice without lawyers.* Cambridge: Cambridge University Press.

Coalition for RECOM (2011). *Proposed RECOM statute.* Retrieved from http://www.recom.link/about-us-2/sta-je-rekom/

Cohen, B. (1993, April/May). Why Europe failed to halt the genocide in Bosnia. *Washington Report on Middle East Affairs, 39.*

Collaku, P. (2015, October 22). Kosovo, Montenegro sign deal on missing persons. *BalkanInsight.* Retrieved from http://www.balkaninsight.com/en/article/kosovo-montenegro-reach-agreement-on-missing-person-s-10-22-2015

Cruvellier, T., & Valiñas, M. (2006). *Croatia: Selected developments in transitional justice* [Briefing paper]. Available from https://www.ictj.org/publication/croatia-selected-developments-transitional-justice

Daalder, I. H. (2000). *Getting to Dayton: The making of America's Bosnia policy.* Washington, DC: Brookings Institution Press.

Đilas, A. (1995, July/August). Tito's last secret: How did he keep the Yugoslavs together? *Foreign Affairs.* Retrieved from http://www.foreignaffairs.com/articles /51216/aleksa-Đilas/tito-s-last-secret-how-did-he-keep-the-yugoslavs-together

Documenta, Humanitarian Law Center, & Research and Documentation Center Sarajevo. (2006). Transitional justice in post-Yugoslav countries: Report for 2006. Retrieved from http://wcjp.unicri.it/proceedings/docs/DOCUMENTA-HLC-RCS_Trans%20justice%20in%20ex%20Yu%20countries_2006_eng.PDF

Domin, T. (2001). History of Bosnia and Herzegovina from the origins to 1992. Reprint of *SFOR Informer, 122*(122). Retrieved from http://www.nato.int/sfor/indexinf/122/p03a/t0103a.htm

Duthie, R. (2009, November). Building Trust and Capacity: Civil Society and Transitional Justice from a Development Perspective (Publication). Retrieved November 11, 2017, from International Center for Transitional Justice website: https://www.ictj.org/publication/building-trust-and-capacity-civil-society-and-transitional-justice-development-0

Dvořáková, V. (2007). Introduction. In V. Dvořáková & A. Milardović (Eds.), *Lustration and consolidation of democracy and the rule of law in Central and Eastern Europe* (pp. 11-15). Zagreb: CPI.

Dvořáková, V., & Milardović, A. (Eds.). (2007). *Lustration and consolidation of democracy and the rule of law in Central and Eastern Europe.* Zagreb: CPI.

Džidić, D. (2012, October 9). *Bosnia's Transitional Justice Strategy requires political support.* Retrieved from http://www.transconflict.com/2012/10/bosnias-transitional-justice-strategy-requires-political-support-090/

Džidić, D. (2014, October 14). Bosnia struggles with war crimes investigation backlog. *BalkanInsight.* Retrieved from http://www.balkaninsight.com/en/article/bosnia-failing-to-reduce-number-of-war-crimes-investigations

Fischer, M. (2011). Transitional justice and reconciliation: Theory and practice. In B. Austin, M. Fischer, & H.-J. Giessmann (Eds.), *Advancing conflict transformation: The Berghof handbook II* (pp. 406-424). Opladen: Barbara Budrich.

Fisher, M., & Petrović-Ziemer, L. (2013). Dealing with the Past in the Western Balkans (Rep. No. 18). Berlin: Berghof Foundation.

Friedman, A. B. (2013). Transitional Justice and Local Ownership: A Framework for the Protection of Human Rights. Akron law Review, 46(3). doi:10.2139/ssrn.1919874

Friends Committee on National Legislation [FCNL]. (1999, July). *A brief history of Yugoslavia.* Retrieved from http://fcnl.org/resources/newsletter/jul99/a_brief_history_of_yugoslavia/

Gates, S., Binningsbø, H. M., & Lie, T. G. (2007). *Post-conflict justice and sustainable peace.* Washington, DC: The World Bank.

Global Information Society Watch. (2011). Bosnia and Herzegovina (Rep.). Global Information Society Watch.

Haider, H. (2016). Transitional justice: Topic guide. Birmingham, UK: GSDRC, University of Birmingham.

Hoare, M. A. (2008, December). *From Nuremberg to the International Criminal Tribunal for the former Yugoslavia.* Retrieved from http://www.bosnia.org.uk/news /news_body.cfm?newsid=2530

Holbrooke, R. C. (1998). *End to a war.* New York: Random House.

Hrlović, D. (2013). Public Legal Education in Bosnia and Herzegovina: Overview of Needs, Opportunities, and Capacities (Rep.). Sarajevo: Analitika – Center for Social Research.

Human Rights Watch. (1995). *The Human Rights Watch global report on women's human rights.* Retrieved from https://www.hrw.org/legacy/about/projects/womrep/

Human Rights Watch. (2017, January 13). Bosnia and Herzegovina. Retrieved November 08, 2017, from https://www.hrw.org/world-report/2017/country-chapters/bosnia-and-herzegovina

International Center for Transitional Justice [ICTJ]. (2006). *The Tribunal's accomplishments in justice and law.* Retrieved from http://www.icty.org/x/file/Outreach/view_from_hague/jit_accomplishmen ts_en.pdf

International Center for Transitional Justice. (2007). Reparations in Theory and Practice (Reparative Justice Series, Publication). New York, NY: International Center for Transitional Justice.

International Center for Transitional Justice [ICTJ]. (2009). *What is transitional justice?* Retrieved from https://www.ictj.org/sites/default/files/ICTJ-Global-Transitional-Justice-2009-English.pdf

International Center for Transitional Justice. (2018). Institutional Reform. Retrieved April 26, 2018, from https://www.ictj.org/our-work/transitional-justice-issues/institutional-reform

International Criminal Court for the Former Yugoslavia. (1995). *The tribunal's accomplishments: injustice and law* [Press release]. Den Hague, Netherlands: International Criminal Court for the Former Yugoslavia.

International Criminal Tribunal for the Former Yugoslavia. (2010). *About the ICTY.* Retrieved from http://www.icty.org/en/about

International Criminal Court for the Former Yugoslavia. (2017, November). Infographic: ICTY Facts & Figures. Retrieved December 26, 2017, from http://www.icty.org/en/content/infographic-icty-facts-figures

International Justice Resource Center. (2015, August 25). *Kosovo to create special war crimes court but faces challenges.* Retrieved from http://www.ijrcenter.org/2015/08/25/kosovo-to-create-special-war-crimes-court-but-faces-challenges/

Jović, D. (2009). *Yugoslavia: A state that withered away.* West Lafayette, IN: Purdue University Press.

Kadayifci-Orellana, S. A. (2009). Ethno-religious conflicts: Exploring the role of religion in conflict resolution. In J. Bercovitch, V. A. Kremenyuk, & I. W. Zartman (Eds.), *The SAGE handbook of conflict resolution* (pp. 264-280). London: SAGE.

Kandić, N. (2007, January 22). *Transitional justice in post-conflict societies of former Yugoslavia* [Lecture]. University of Michigan, Ann Arbor, MI. Retrieved from http://www.ii.umich.edu/UMICH/ces/Home/Resources/Michigan%20Pap er%20Series/Kandic_TransitionalJustice.pdf

Kastner, P. (2013). Cyberjustice in the Context of Transitional Justice (Working paper No. 9). Laboratory of Cyberjustice.

Kisić, I. (2013). Transitional Justice in the Western Balkans (Publication). Retrieved http://www.bundesheer.at/pdf_pool/publikationen/transitional_justice_sr _11_2013_05_i_kisic.pdf

Klip, A., & Sluiter, G. (2001). *Annotated cases of leading tribunals.* Antwerp, Belgium: Intersentia.

Kostić, R. (2012). Transitional justice and reconciliation in Bosnia-Herzegovina: Whose memories, whose justice? *Sociologija, 54*(4), 649-666. doi:10.2298/SOC1204649K

Kureljusic, S. (2016, October 04). Bosnia Elects War Criminal, Corrupt Officials as Mayors. Retrieved April 12, 2018, from http://www.balkaninsight.com/en/article/bosnia-elects-war-criminal-corrupt-officials-as-mayors-10-04-2016

Kritiz, N. (2009). Policy implications of empirical research on transitional justice. In H. Van Der Merwe, V. Baxter, & A. R. Chapman (Eds.), *Assessing the impact of transitional justice* (pp. 13-24). Washington, DC: United States Institute of Peace.

Latal, S. (2014, October 10). Bosnia approaches polls with more fear than hope. *BalkanInsight*. Retrieved from http://www.balkaninsight.com/en/article/bosnia-approaches-polls-with-more-fear-than-hope

Lambourne, W. (2003). Post-Conflict Peacebuilding: Meeting Human Needs for Justice and Reconciliation. Journal of Peace, Conflict and Development, (4). doi:10.7246/pcd.0404

Lescure, K. (1996). *International justice for former Yugoslavia: The workings of the International Criminal Tribunal of The Hague*. The Hague, Netherlands: Kluwer Law International.

Llewellyn, J. J., & Howse, R. (1999). Restorative justice: A conceptual framework. *Social Science Research Network*. Retrieved from http://papers.ssrn.com/sol3/papers.cfm?abstract_id=2114291

Lynch, C. (2015, November 22). The Bosnian war cables. *Foreign Policy*. Retrieved from http://foreignpolicy.com/2015/11/22/the-bosnian-war-cables/

Maepa, T. (2005). The truth and reconciliation commission as a model of restorative justice In T. Maepa (Ed.), *Beyond retribution: Prospects for restorative justice in South Africa* (pp. 67-75). Pretoria: Restorative Justice Centre.

Maiese, M. G. (2003, July). *Types of justice*. Retrieved from http://www.beyondintractability.org/essay/types_of_justice/?nid=1013

Malek, C. (2013, May). *Reconciliation*. Retrieved from http://www.beyondintractability.org/coreknowledge/reconciliation

Mallinder, L. (2013). Bosnia-Herzegovina. In L. Stan & N. Nedelsky (Eds.), *Encyclopedia of transitional justice* (pp. 60-67). Cambridge: Cambridge University Press.

Mani, R. (2002). *Beyond retribution: Seeking justice in the shadows of war*. Oxford: Blackwell Publishing.

Meernik, J., & Guerrero, J. R. (2014). Can international criminal justice advance ethnic reconciliation? The ICTY and ethnic relations in Bosnia-Herzegovina. Southeast European and Black Sea Studies, 14(3), 383-407. doi:10.1080/14683857.2014.924675

Milekić, S. (2014, November 18). Regional truth commission one step closer to establishment. *BalkanInsight*. Retrieved from http://www.balkaninsight.com/en/article/transitional-justice-forum-opens-painful-topics

Ministry of Justice of Bosnia and Herzegovina. (2008, December 30). National Strategy for Processing of War Crimes Cases Adopted [Press release]. Retrieved November 07, 2017, from http://www.mpr.gov.ba/aktuelnosti/vijesti/default.aspx?id=573&langTag=en-US

Ministry of Justice of Bosnia and Herzegovina. (2013). Report of BiH Justice Sector Institutions on Implementation of BiH JSRS AP for the period January-June 2013 (Rep.). Sarajevo: Ministry of Justice of Bosnia and Herzegovina.

Mobekk, E. (2005). Transitional justice in post-conflict societies: Approaches to reconciliation. In A. Ebnöther & P. Fluri (Eds.), *After intervention: Public security management in post-conflict societies: From intervention to sustainable local ownership* (pp. 261-292). Geneva: Geneva Centre for Democratic Control of Armed Forces.

Moratti, M., & Sabic-El-Rayess, A. (2009, June). *Transitional justice and DDR: The case of Bosnia and Herzegovina.* New York: International Center for Transitional Justice. Retrieved from https://www.ictj.org/sites/default/files/ICTJ-DDR-Bosnia-CaseStudy-2009-English.pdf

Nickson, R., & Braithwaite, J. (2013). Deeper, broader, longer transitional justice. *European Journal of Criminology, 1*(19), 445-463. doi:10.1177/1477370813505954

Nuremberg Trials. (2010). *Nuremberg trials.* Retrieved from http://www.history.com/topics/world-war-ii/nuremberg-trials

Obradovic, S., & Howarth, C. (2016). Everyday Reconciliation. In The Social Psychology of Everyday Politics. Routledge: London.

Orlović, S. (2013). Transitional Justice in Post-Yugoslav Countries Report for 2010 - 2011 (Publication). Belgrade: Humanitarian Law Center.

Office of the United Nations High Commissioner for Human Rights. (2009). Retrieved December 27, 2017, from Rule-of-Law Tools for Post-Conflict states: Amnesties: http://www.ohchr.org/Documents/Publications/Amnesties_en.pdf

Office of the United Nations Comissioner for Human Rights. (2009). Rule-of-Law Tools for Post-Conflict States National Consultations on Transitional Justice (Publication). Geneva and New York: United Nations.

Olsen, T. D., Payne, L. A., & Reiter, A. G. (2010). *Transitional justice in balance: Comparing processes, weighing efficacy.* Washington, DC: United States Institute of Peace.

Ozturk, T. (2014, November 23). Bosnia: Challenges remain 19 years after Dayton accord. *Anadolou Agency.* Retrieved from http://aa.com.tr/en/politics/bosnia-challenges-remain-19-years-after-dayton-accord/98948

Palmer, N., Viebach, J., Jones, B., Norridge, Z., Grant, A., Patel, A., Ferguson, P. (2013). *Transitional justice methods manual.* Bern, Switzerland: Swiss Peace. Retrieved from http://www.swisspeace.ch/fileadmin/user_upload/Media/Publications/TJ_Methods_Manual_homepage.pdf

Palmer, P. (2004). History. In I. Bell (Ed.), *Central and South-Eastern Europe 2004* (4th ed., pp. 109-114). Baltimore: Europa Publications.

Parish, M. (2012, April 9). Two decades on, Bosnia's divisions are self-imposed. *BalkanInsight.* Retrieved from http://www.balkaninsight.com/en/article/two-decades-on-bosnia-s-divisions-are-self-imposed

Pham, P., & Vinck, P. (2007). Empirical research and the development and assessment of transitional justice mechanisms. *International Journal of Transitional Justice, 1*(2), 231-248. doi:10.1093/ijtj/ijm017

Pinson, M. (Ed.). (2007). *The muslims of Bosnia and Herzegovina: Their historic development from the Middle Ages to the dissolution of Yugoslavia* (2nd ed.). Boston, MA: Harvard University Press.

Powers, S. E. (2011). Rwanda's gacaca courts: Implications for international criminal law and transitional justice. *Insight, 15*(17). Retrieved from https://www.asil.org/insights/volume/15/issue/17/rwanda%E2%80%99s-gacaca-courts-implications-international-criminal-law-and

Prison Fellowship International. (n.d). *What is restorative justice?* Retrieved July 4, 2010 from http://www.pfi.org/cjr/downloads/focus-on-justice/focus-on-justice/what-is-restorative-justice/view

Ramsbotham, O., Miall, H., & Woodhouse, T. (2005). *Contemporary conflict resolution: The prevention, management and transformation of deadly conflicts* (2nd ed.). Cambridge, UK: Polity.

Rangelov, I., & Theros, M. (2007, November). *Maintaining the process in Bosnia and Herzegovina: Coherence and complementarity of EU institutions and civil society in the field of transitional justice.* Bonn, Germany: Working Group on Development and Peace. Retrieved from http://reliefweb.int/sites/reliefweb.int/files/resources/557E443C4E849C51492574B4001EDBEA-Full_Report.pdf

Ristić, M. (2015, December 14). Serbia unveils first-ever war crimes strategy. *Balkan Insight.* Retrieved from http://www.balkaninsight.com/en/article/serbia-publishes-war-crimes-strategy-12-13-2015

Roht-Arriaza, N. (2006). The new landscape of transitional justice. In N. Arriaza-Rhot & J. Mariezcurrena (Eds.), *Transitional justice in the twenty-first century* (pp. 1-16). Cambridge, UK: Cambridge University Press.

Roos, S. (2007). Preface. In V. Dvořáková & A. Milardović (Eds.), *Lustration and consolidation of democracy and the rule of law in Central and Eastern Europe* (pp. 7-10). Zagreb: CPI.

Shuttenberg, F. (2008). *How can retributive justice foster reconciliation?: On the impact of international and hybrid criminal tribunals, the ICC as a potential successor and arising consequences for Europe* (Master's thesis, University of Twente, Weimar, Germany). Retrieved from http://essay.utwente.nl/57962/

Sriram, C. L., & Pillay, S. (2010). *Peace versus justice?: The dilemma of transitional justice in Africa.* Oxford: James Currey.

Steflja, I. (2012, January 6). Challenges of transitional justice in Rwanda. *Africa Portal.* Retrieved from https://www.africaportal.org/dspace/articles/challenges-transitional-justice-rwanda

Stone, D., Patton, B., & Sheen, S. (2000). *Difficult conversations: How to discuss what matters most.* New York: Penguin.

Stover, E., Megally, H., & Mufti, H. (2005). Bremer's "gordian knot": Transitional justice and the US occupation of Iraq. *Human Rights Quarterly, 27*(3), 830-857.

Stover, E., & Weinstein, H. M. (2004). *My neighbor, my enemy: Justice and community in the aftermath of mass atrocity.* Cambridge, UK: Cambridge University Press.

Taylor, A. (2015, July 9). 20 years since the Srebrenica massacre. *The Atlantic.* Retrieved from http://www.theatlantic.com/photo/2015/07/20-years-since-the-srebrenica-massacre/398135/

Tolbert, D. (2014, April 3). *Transitional justice should be part of Serbia's accession to the EU.* Retrieved from https://www.ictj.org/news/transitional-justice-serbia

Tomović, D. (2015, May 12). Montenegro must tackle war crimes, chief prosecutor says. *BalkanInsight.* Retrieved from http://www.balkaninsight.com/en/article /montenegro-needs-to-tackle-war-crimes-chief-prosecutor-says

United Nations. (2010, April 10). Guidance Note of the Secretary-General: United Nations Approach to Transitional Justice (Publication). Retrieved November 16, 2017, from United Nations website: https://www.un. org/ruleoflaw/blog/doc ument/guidance-note-of-the-secretary-general-united-nations-approach-to-transitional-justice/

United Nations Development Programme Bosnia and Herzegovina. (2011, April 20). Facing the Past and Access to Justice from A Public Perspective Special Report (Rep.). Retrieved August 8, 2015, from United Nations Development Programme Bosnia and Herzegovina website: http://www.ba.undp.org/content/bosnia_and_herzegovina/en/home/libra ry/crisis_prevention_and_recovery/facing-the-past-and-access-to-justice.html

United Nations Resident Coordinator Office in Bosnia and Herzegovina, 2013. (n.d.). Public Opinion Poll Analytical Report (Rep.). Sarajevo: United Nations Resident Coordinator Office in Bosnia and Herzegovina.

University of Ulster Transitional Justice Institute. (2015). *Research theme* (Theory, method and evaluation section). Retrieved from http://www.ulster.ac.uk/research-and-innovation/research-institutes/transitional-justice-institute/research/research-themes

Van Der Velden, M. (2010). Transitional justice in Bosnia and Herzegovina: Tiny steps forward. *Effectius Newsletter,* 9. Retrieved from http://effectius.com/yahoo_site_admin/assets/docs/TransitionalJusticeinB osniaandHerzegovinatinastepsfor-ward_Maurice_Newsletter9_WDW.301102451.pdf

Vinck, P., & Pham, P. N. (2010). Outreach Evaluation: The International Criminal Court in the Central African Republic. International Journal of Transitional Justice, 4(3), 421-442. doi:10.1093/ijtj/ijq014

Watkins, M. (2003). Strategic simplification: Toward a theory of modular design in negotiation. *International Negotiations, 8*(1), 149-167. http://dx.doi.org/10.1163/138234003769590695

Weitekamp, E. (1993). Reparative justice: Towards a victim oriented system. European Journal on Criminal Policy and Research, 1,1 70-93.

Wheeling Jesuit University Center for Educational Technologies. (2002). *Bosnia within Yugoslavia, 1918-1992.* Retrieved from http://www.cotf.edu/earthinfo/balkans/bosnia/BNtopic3.html

Wilkes, G., Kuburić, A., Andrejč, G., Kuburić, Z., Brkić, M., Jusić, M., & Momčinović, Z. P. (2012). *Reconciliation and trust building in Bosnia-Herzegovina: A survey of popular attitudes in four cities and regions* [Scholarly project]. Retrieved from http://malikoraci.com.ba/wp-content/uploads/2012/11/Edinburg-Eng-FINAL-reduced-1.pdf

Zartman, W. (2003, August). *Ripeness.* Retrieved from http://www.beyondintractability.org/essay/ripeness

Zehr, H., & Mika, H.(1998). Fundamental concepts of restorative justice *Contemporary Justice Review, 1,* 47-55.

Appendix A: Study Participation Letter

Title of Study: Strategizing Justice: A Critical Analysis of Bosnia and Herzegovina's Draft Transitional Justice Strategy and its ability to foster Reconciliation

Principal investigator: Jared O. Bell

Co-investigator: Ismael Muvingi, Ph.D.

Institutional Review Board:

Nova Southeastern University

Office of Grants and Contracts

(954) 262-5369/Toll Free: 866-499-0790

IRB@nsu.nova.edu

Site Information: www.surveymonkey.com

Description of Study: This research project is being conducted by Jared Bell of Nova Southeastern University. The objective of this research project is to attempt to understand if the national draft Transitional Justice Strategy will foster reconciliation in Bosnia and Herzegovina. The survey is being given to residents in 3 cities (Mostar, Sarajevo, and Banja Luka) online.

Risks/Benefits to the Participant: There are no known risks if you decide to participate in this research study, nor are there any costs for participating in the study. The information you provide will help me understand transitional justice and reconciliation and Bosnia and Herzegovina. The information collected may not benefit you directly, but what I learn from this study should provide general benefits to employees, companies, and researchers.

Cost and Payments to the Participant: There is no cost for participation in this study. Participation is completely voluntary and no payment will be provided.

Confidentiality: This survey is anonymous. If you choose to participate, you will not be asked to write your name on the questionnaire. No one will be able to identify you. No one will know whether you participated in this study.

Participant's Right to Withdraw from the Study: You have the right to refuse to participate in this study and the right to withdraw from the study at any time without penalty.

I have read this letter and I fully understand the contents of this document and voluntarily consent to participate. All of my questions concerning this research have been answered. If I have any questions in the future about this study, they will be answered by the investigator listed above or his/her staff.

I understand that the completion of this questionnaire implies my consent to participate in this study. If you want to continue on with the survey please click yes below.

Appendix B: Pismo učešća u studiji

Naziv studije: Strategizacija pravde: kritička analiza nacrta Strategije tranzicijske pravde Bosne i Hercegovine i njegova sposobnost da podstakne pomirenje

Glavni istraživač: Jared O. Bell

Suistraživač: Ismael Muvingi, Ph.D.

Institucionalni Odbor za pregled:

Nova Southeastern University

Ured za grantove i ugovore

(954) 262-5369 / Besplatna linija: 866-499-0790

IRB@nsu.nova.edu

Naziv website-a: www.surveymonkey.com

Opis studije: Ovaj istraživački projekt provodi Jared Bell s Nova Southeastern University. Cilj ovog istraživačkog projekta je da pokuša da shvati da li će nacrt nacionalne Strategije tranzicijske pravde podstaći pomirenje u Bosni i Herecgovini. Anketu popunjavaju stanovnici tri grada (Mostar, Sarajevo i Banja Luka) online.

Rizici/Koristi za učesnike: Ne postoje poznati rizici ako se odlučite da učestvujete u ovoj istraživačkoj studiji, niti postoje bilo kakvi troškovi učešća u studiji. Informacije koje mi pružite će mi pomoći da razumijem tranzicijsku pravdu i pomirenje i Bosnu i Hercegovinu. Možda nećete imati direktnu korist od prikupljenih informacija, ali ono što ću saznati iz ove studije treba pružiti opću korist uposlenicima, kompanijama, i istraživačima.

Troškovi i naknade učesnicima: Ne postoje troškovi učešća u ovoj studiji. Učešće je potpuno dobrovoljno i naknada neće biti obezbijeđena.

Povjerljivost: Ova anketa je anonimna. Ako se odlučite učestvovati, neće Vam biti traženo da napišete svoje ime u upitniku. Niko Vas neće moći identifikovati. Niko neće znati da ste učestvovali u ovoj studiji.

Učesnikovo pravo da se povuče iz studije: Imate pravo da odbijete učestvovati u ovoj studiji i pravo da se bilo kada povučete iz studije, bez kazne.

Pročitao/la sam ovo pismo i u potpunosti razumijem sadržaj ovog dokumenta, i dobrovoljno pristajem da učestvujem. Na sva moja pitanja u vezi ovog istraživanja je odgovoreno. Ako budem imao/la bilo kakvih pitanja u budućnosti o ovoj studiji, ona će biti odgovorena od strane gore navedenog istraživača ili njegovog/njenog osoblja.

Appendix C: Recruitment Statement

Do you have an opinion on justice and moving beyond the past in Bosnia? If so we want your Opinion!!! Please proceed to the survey link below!

The government of Bosnia and Herzegovina's proposed National Transitional Strategy is a comprehensive framework for dealing with the legacy of human rights violations and war crimes, to build the foundations of a peaceful future. The hope of this Strategy is to foster some type of reconciliation from the brutality of the past. The purpose of this survey is to gauge your opinion as to whether or not you believe the Strategy proposed can help foster any sense of reconciliation among the Bosnian populace? This survey is being collected in part of data for dissertation research. Your opinion is valued and much appreciated! Thank You for your participation.

Appendix D: Izjava o učešću

Da li imate mišljenje o pravdi i odmaku od prošlosti u Bosni? Ako je tako, želimo znati Vaše mišljenje!!! Molimo slijedite link za anketu ispod!

Vlasti Bosne i Hercegovine su predložile nacionalnu Strategiju tranzicijske pravde kao sveobuhvatan okvir za suočavanje s nasljeđem kršenja ljudskih prava i ratnih zločina, s ciljem građenja temelja za mirnu budućnost. Nada ove Strategije je da će iznjedriti neki oblik pomirenja iz brutalnosti prošlosti. Svrha ove ankete je da procijeni Vaše mišljenje o tome da li vjerujete ili ne da predložena Strategija može iznjedriti neki oblik pomirenja među narodima Bosne i Hercegovine. Ova anketa je dio istraživanja za disertaciju. Vaše mišljenje se vrednuje i veoma cijeni! Hvala Vam na učešću.

Appendix E: Survey A

Transitional Justice Strategy and Reconciliation Research Survey

Bosnia and Herzegovina's proposed National Transitional Justice Strategy is a comprehensive framework for dealing with the legacy of human rights violations and war crimes, to build the foundations of a peaceful future. The hope of this Strategy is to foster some type of reconciliation from the brutality of the past. This purpose of this survey is to gauge your opinion as to whether or not you believe the Strategy proposed can help foster any sense of reconciliation among the Bosnian populace? This survey is being collected in part of data for dissertation research. Thank You for your participation!

Researcher:

Jared O. Bell, Ph.D. Candidate

Nova Southeastern University

Department of Conflict Resolution

1. **Are you familiar with the proposed Transitional Justice Strategy?**

□ Yes   □ No

2. **If so how did you learn about it?**

□ Television   □ Newspaper   □ Internet   □ Politician/ Political Party

3. **The strategy focuses on 5 key areas for addressing the conflict in the 1990s: truth and fact finding, reparations, rehabilitation, memorialization, and institutional reform. Do you think these areas address the main issues that have stopped Bosnia and Herzegovina from moving on?**

□ Yes   □ No

4. **Do you think the above processes are needed for Bosnia and Herzegovina to move forward from its past?**

□ Yes   □ No

5. **What of the five processes do you think is the most important out of the 5 key areas mentioned in question 3 to help Bosnia and Herzegovina move on from the past? Check more than one if it applies.**

□ Truth and Fact finding   □ Reparations   □ Rehabilitations

□ Memorialization   □ Political Reform

6. **Do you think moving beyond the past is possible period in Bosnia and Herzegovina?**

□ Yes   □ No

7. **If you believe moving on is possible, do you have faith in the Bosnian government to lead the efforts to move on?**

□ Yes   □ No

8. **Will activities in these key areas impact you or your family personally? If yes, which one's? Check more than one if more than one applies.**

□ Yes   □ No

□ Truth and Fact   □ Reparations   □ Rehabilitation   □ Memorialization
finding

9. **Will participating in any of the above activities or receiving any of benefits help you personally be able to help you accept the past and move on?**

□ Yes, Completely   □ Yes, eventually   □ No, I'll never be able to move on

10. **Which city do you live in?**

□ Sarajevo   □ Mostar   □ Banja Luka

11. **What ethnicity do you consider yourself?**

□ Bosniak   □ Croat   □ Serb   □ Other

12. **What is your gender?**

□ Male   □ Female

13. **What is your age range?**

□ 18-24   □ 25-33   □ 33-44   □ 45-54

□ 55-65   □ 66 and older

Appendix F: Survey B

Strategija tranzicijske pravde i anketa o istraživanju pomirenja

Bosanskohercegovačka predložena nacionalna Strategija tranzicijske pravde je sveobuhvatan okvir za suočavanje s nasljeđem kršenja ljudskih prava i ratnih zločina, s ciljem građenja temelja za mirnu budućnost. Nada ove Strategije je da će iznjedriti neki oblik pomirenja iz brutalnosti prošlosti. Svrha ove ankete je da procijeni Vaše mišljenje o tome da li vjerujete ili ne da predložena Strategija može iznjedriti neki oblik pomirenja među narodima Bosne i Hercegovine. Ova anketa je dio istraživanja za disertaciju. Hvala Vam na učešću!

Istraživač:

Jared O. Bell, Ph.D. kandidat

Nova Southeastern University

Odsjek za rješavanje konflikata

1. **Da li ste upoznati sa Strategijom tranzicijske pravde?**

□ Da   □ Ne

2. **Ako jeste upoznati, kako ste saznali za nju?**

□ Televizija   □ Novine   □ Internet   □ Političari/Politička stranka

3. **Strategija se fokusira na 5 ključnih oblasti koji se odnose na sukobe iz 1990-ih: istinu i iznalaženje činjenica, reparaciju, rehabilitaciju, memorijalizaciju i institucijske reforme. Da li mislite da te oblasti pokrivaju glavne probleme zbog kojih Bosna i Hercegovina ne može krenuti naprijed?**

□ Da   □ Ne

4. **Da li mislite da su gore spomenuti procesi potrebni Bosni i Hercegovini da krene naprijed i prevaziđe svoju prošlost?**

□ Da   □ Ne

5. **Koji je od pet procesa spomenutih u pitanju 3, po Vama, najbitniji za Bosnu i Hercegovinu kako bi prevazišla svoju prošlost? Možete označiti više od jednog polja u odgovorima.**

☐ Istina i iznalaženje činjenica   ☐ Kompenzacije   ☐ Rehabilitacije

☐ Sjećanje   ☐ Institucionalne reforme

6. **Da li mislite da je prevazilaženje prošlosti moguće u Bosni i Hercegovini?**

☐ Da   ☐ Ne

7. **Ako mislite da jeste, da li imate povjerenje u vlasti Bosne i Hercegovine da će uložiti napor da BiH krene naprijed?**

☐ Da   ☐ Ne

8. **Da li će aktivnosti u ovim ključnim oblastima utjecati na Vas i Vašu porodicu/obitelj? Ako da, koje? Označite više od jedne ako se odnose na Vas.**

☐ Da   ☐ Ne

☐ Istina i iznalaženje činjenica   ☐ Kompenzacija   ☐ Rehabilitacija   ☐ Sjećanje

9. **Da li će Vam učestvovanje u bilo kojoj od gore navedenih aktivnosti pomoći da prihvatite prošlost i krenete dalje?**

☐ Da, u poptupnosti   ☐ Da, s vremenom   ☐ Ne, nikada neću moći prihvatiti prošlost i krenuti dalje

10. **U kojem gradu živite?**

☐ Sarajevo   ☐ Mostar   ☐ Banja Luka

11. **Kojoj etničkoj skupini pripadate?**

☐ Bošnjak/inja   ☐ Hrvat/ica   ☐ Srbin/kinja   ☐ Ostali

12. **Koji je Vaš spol?**

☐ Muško   ☐ Žensko

13. **Koliko Vam je godina?**

☐ 18-24   ☐ 25-33   ☐ 33-44   ☐ 45-54

☐ 55-65   ☐ 66 i starije

Index

U